PRAISE FOR

BRANDING FAITH

Through his decades in the media industry, Phil has discovered keys to help leaders expand ministry effectively while using the best of contemporary media resources. *Branding Faith* will impact many with wisdom that will help them maintain substance and integrity in character as they represent the Savior to the masses.

DR. JACK W. HAYFORD
Chancellor, The King's College and Seminary
Founding Pastor, The Church On The Way

Branding Faith is filled with the keen insights of today's dynamic media environment that has made Phil Cooke a trusted media advisor to Joel Osteen and Lakewood Church for more than 25 years. The principles found in this book will change the way you think about your audience and enable you to tell your story more effectively.

DONALD ILOFF, JR.
Senior Advisor and Chief of Communications, Joel Osteen Ministries

Phil Cooke's ideas about branding helped us to completely rethink our global media outreach at Joyce Meyer Ministries. Rebranding this ministry has completely transformed the way we connect with our audience. Whatever you think you know about using the media will change when you read *Branding Faith*.

DAN MEYER
CEO, Joyce Meyer Ministries

At *The Hour of Power* television broadcast, we understand how the media landscape is changing. That's why Phil's advice is so important. In today's media-dominated culture, it is more important than ever that we realize what it takes to get our story heard. If you want to make an impact, this is the book to read.

ROBERT A. SCHULLER
Senior Pastor, The Crystal Cathedral and *The Hour of Power*

Every major corporation in America understands the power of branding
getting your message out, breaking through the mass-marketing o
slaught and clutter, connecting to a target and creating an emotion
attachment. These same principles can be applied to ministry. Phil gets i
Understand the possibilities and unleash the power!

SIMON SWART
Executive Vice President/General Manager, Fox Home Entertainment

The media world is changing faster than any time in history. This boo
is a roadmap for reaching the next generation. For-profit or nonprof
and whatever the size of your company, organization or project, I gua
antee this book will transform your thinking about using the media i
the twenty-first century.

RALPH WINTER
Producer *X-Men, Fantastic Four* and *Planet of the Apes*

BRANDING FAITH

WHY SOME CHURCHES AND NONPROFITS IMPACT CULTURE AND OTHERS DON'T

PHIL COOKE

Regal
From Gospel Light
Ventura, California, U.S.A.

Published by Regal
From Gospel Light
Ventura, California, U.S.A.
www.regalbooks.com
Printed in the U.S.A.

Library of Congress Cataloging-in-Publication Data
Cooke, Phil.
Branding faith : why some ministries impact culture and others don't / Phil Cooke.
p. cm.
ISBN 978-0-8307-4563-0 (hard cover)
1. Christianity—Influence. 2. Civilization, Western. 3. Culture.
4. Church work. I. Title.
BR115.C5C58 2007
269'.2—dc22
2007029537

1 2 3 4 5 6 7 8 9 10 / 10 09 08

CONTENTS

ACKNOWLEDGMENTS

I discovered the information in this book over a long career and with the help of a number of wonderful clients who allowed me the creative space to experiment, learn and grow. To all my faith-based and nonprofit clients, I'm grateful for your encouragement and inspiration over the years.

I also want to thank my incredible team at Cooke Pictures who have provided the support, motivation and ideas that have made a dramatic difference for our clients.

Bucky Rosenbaum, my agent, helped me believe there was an audience that needed to hear this information. His guidance and counsel made the project happen.

Finally, I'm grateful to my brilliant wife, Kathleen, and daughters, Kelsey and Bailey, who have allowed me the freedom to travel and, more important, given me a fantastic reason to come back home.

Phil Cooke
November 1, 2007

PROLOGUE

RESPONDING TO A MEDIA-DRIVEN CULTURE

Men of Issachar, who understood the times and knew what Israel should do.
1 CHRONICLES 12:32

O ye hypocrites, ye can discern the face of the sky; but can ye not discern the signs of the times?
MATTHEW 16:3, *KJV*

My wife, Kathleen, and I were enjoying a relaxing weekend retreat with some friends in the entertainment industry when someone asked an intriguing question: Why do so many Christians do such a terrible job of presenting their message to the world?

As a producer and director in the industry, who also works as a consultant and writer on issues of media and faith, I encounter that question on a pretty frequent basis. In a country where pastors used to be high on the credibility scale, today it seems as if they've fallen nearly to the level of con artists. This postmodern generation has grown up watching endless fights about religion and politics, culture bashing and a host of other ideological battles, and most are, frankly, tired of the brawl. Across the spectrum, organized religious faith has taken a beating in the public square. As a result, *how unbelievers perceive the Christian community could use a little help.*

I answered my friend's question by sharing a passionate belief that in a media-driven culture, we need to do a better job of telling our story. In essence, we need to understand the power of branding and identity, and seriously reconsider how we express our faith to a skeptical and unbelieving world.

One member of the group that weekend, a brilliant writer and producer of big-budget comedy movies who is also a very serious believer, began to turn pale. He turned to me (almost in disgust) and said, "I don't think you could have said anything that would have hurt me more. The idea that we should reduce Christianity to a 'brand' is completely offensive."

A similar event happened a few weeks later, when an online blogger found an advertisement for a lecture I was giving on branding Christian organizations. He posted the ad on his website and proceeded to rip apart the concept that someone could "brand the Christian faith." He considered it cheap and sleazy to even consider such an insulting idea.

After those two events, both driven by well-meaning people, *I realized that I had a branding problem of my own.*

In today's world, the concept of branding carries a lot of negative baggage. As I'll point out later in this book, many people associate branding with much of the criticism and condemnation they hear about the "evils" of corporate America. From environmental destruction, rampant consumerism, globalism, destruction of local cultures, rising personal debt and more, the word "branding" has become an ugly catch-all term that covers just about anything distasteful or extreme about big business.

The truth is, branding isn't about crass commercialism, manipulation, corporate abuses or bad advertising. The AIGA Center for Brand Experience calls it simply, "A person's perception of a product, service, experience, or organization." I prefer to call it "the *story* that surrounds a product, service, person or organization." In other words:

What do people think of when they think of you, your product or your organization?

As I'll explain in much greater detail later in the book, the issue is ultimately about *perception*—how your customer, audience, donor, supporter or even church member perceives his or her experience with your organization. For the purposes of this book, we'll focus on how people perceive their encounters with a local church; a ministry; a religious media program; a nonprofit and humanitarian organization, college or university; or any other religious or nonprofit outreach, including the products and experiences they create.

To attempt to "re-brand" the Christian faith itself would be absurd. As James Twitchell, in his book *Branded Nation,* states, God is a *belief,* not a *brand.*[1] The Christian faith in particular has done very well on its own for the last 2,000 years. It has literally transformed the West and created orphanages, hospitals, universities and countless humanitarian outreaches. Biblical references fill the pages of our greatest books; music, art, and literature would be poor indeed without its remarkable influence. Argue all you want about the belief itself, but there's no question that Christianity has been a powerful force that has changed the world.

However, at this particular moment in history, I propose that we need to dramatically change the way we publicly *express* that belief. A critical key to accomplishing that goal is *branding.*

Throughout the history of the Church, leaders and communicators of the faith have struggled against the various cultures in which they found themselves. During the dangerous days of the Early Church, the apostles lived and worked against the backdrop of the Roman occupation of the Middle East.

Others since then have struggled against cultures of discrimination, hostility and outright violence; and even today, many Christians in different countries continue to express their faith under the looming threat of arrest and execution.

During some centuries, the Christian faith was virtually a *civil* religion. We now look back at what we call Christendom—when Christianity was as much a social and political force as a religious issue. By contrast, my father was a pastor during the fifties and sixties when the debate wasn't about the *influence* of God but about the *death* of God. In every case, just as Paul did in the New Testament, recorded in Acts 17, anyone who attempted to present the Christian message in a relevant way knew they had to recognize and understand the cultural framework of the time in order to be an effective communicator.

Media Is Culture

Today, the Church in the West struggles under a different framework: *the power of global media*. As I'll show later in the book, the media's influence in our lives is pervasive. Education, business, religion, leisure and even family life are all measured against that influence.

The answer to "Who's influencing the Church today?" is the same as "Who's influencing the culture?"

It's the media.

That's why our challenge today is how to express our faith in a media-dominated culture. How do we tell our story alongside the maddening swirl of TV, radio, computer, digital music player, Internet, cell phone and other technologies competing for our attention? Throughout the book, I'll call these things "clutter."

How do we get our message heard through the massive and growing amount of media static out there?

Stay tuned.

LOSING OUR VOICE

What does religion look like from a marketing point of view? Mind you, I'm not talking about God. That's a belief, not a brand. A brand is a story that travels with a product or service or, in this case, a concept. In the beginning of Christianity was the Word, and, as I'm sure you've already guessed, the Word was the Brand.

JAMES B. TWITCHELL, *BRANDED NATION*[1]

My team gets hired when a church, ministry or nonprofit organization has lost its voice.

Perhaps you've experienced a similar situation: In spite of doing great works in the community, like building homeless shelters, drug treatment centers or food banks, your organization still lives hand to mouth. Or, as a pastor or religious leader who has had a genuine calling, you have built a great team, invested your life in the vision with powerful preaching, teaching or ministry, but the spark never happens; growth never takes off or it just suddenly stops.

After years or decades of work, nobody seems to care. You've lost your impact and lost your voice to the very people with whom you're trying to communicate.

I see it happen all too often: Media ministries that just can't seem to grow beyond a local broadcast; churches that hit a ceiling on adding members; humanitarian outreaches that can't seem to break through a certain level of fund-raising.

In most cases they are led by qualified, sincere men and women, and almost all have a strong vision for excellence. They spend money on capital campaigns, media equipment, church-growth consultants, marketing, TV or radio time, advertising campaigns and more, but they just seem trapped and unable to grow beyond a certain point.

They're just not getting their message across.

A number of years ago, I was invited to the monthly creative and marketing meeting for one of the largest Christian media ministries in the world. The media-buying company had actually asked me to come because, for some time, they had noticed that the television viewers—although historically a large audience—had stopped growing. Once they began investigating, they discovered it was pretty much the same story throughout the entire ministry. Income had hit a plateau, product sales were flat, television response was slowing, and partnership was almost nonexistent.

When I was introduced to the ministry leader—a prominent religious leader—his first response was, "Well, I don't know why you're here. There's nothing wrong with this organization."

The media buyer tried to explain that because of my work with a number of the largest nonprofit organizations in the country, I might offer them some advice on how to break through the ceiling they had hit.

His response was blunt. "I watch lots of religious television, and our program is as good as anything I see out there. I don't know how you could possibly help us."

The room got a bit icy, and it felt like the temperature was dropping quickly.

I stood up and walked around the room. In a respectful tone, I replied, "I think you're absolutely correct. Your program is well produced and your ministry has always been very popular. But the truth is, you've suddenly hit a wall that no one seems to be able to explain." (His program did have some issues, but nothing insurmountable.)

I continued, "Before I came to this meeting, I spent time studying the different expressions of the ministry, and the first thing I noticed was that everything you do looks different from everything else."

I pulled out pictures of the ministry website, the title card from the opening of the television program, some recent DVD product sets, a print ad, a brochure and his latest book. I then pointed out that they all looked like they came from five or six different organizations. There was no common look or theme to anything—they all appeared to be designed by six different artists. Essentially, they were telling six different (and sometimes conflicting) stories about the ministry.

The Power of Unifying the Story

"This organization doesn't convey a unified look and feel," I said. "The TV program looks different from the website, which looks different from your books and tapes, which look different from your ministry magazine. When you look at the advertising from a major brand like Nike, Starbucks or Apple Computer, everything they do—from bus stop ads, to television, to magazines—has a common look and style. They carry the theme of the company across all media, which in turn strengthens the power of the company in the minds of the consumer."

I got his attention.

"So how do we fix that?" he asked.

"Tell me who you are," I replied.

"We're a teaching ministry that's called to preach and teach the message of Jesus Christ."

I urged him to be more specific, saying, "That's no different from a million other churches and ministries out there."

"Okay, we're called to television."

"Still no good." I decided to push him a bit. "The question isn't, What do you do? or, How do you do it? The real question here is, Who *are* you?"

He stopped for a second, and I said, "Let me put it this way:

What do people think of when they think of you?"

He had no answer. He'd never thought of it before.

Look around the religious media landscape in this country. There are a lot of choices. You can turn on any religious TV or radio station in America today and hear a multitude of national TV voices like Joel Osteen, Joyce Meyer, Ed Young, John Hagee, Rod Parsley, Charles Stanley, David Jeremiah; or radio voices like James Dobson, John MacArthur, Jack Graham, Chuck Swindoll, Greg Laurie and Beth Moore.

The National Religious Broadcasters—the professional association for religious media ministries—boasts more than 1,400 member organizations. But that's a drop in the bucket compared to the hundreds of thousands of churches and ministries across the country and around the globe.

It's no different in the nonprofit world. Museums, homeless shelters, after-school programs, universities and more are all driven by the ability to raise funding. But how do you stand out in your community?

The problem is not just about particularly large organizations. In fact, it's often especially critical in local, neighborhood churches or small nonprofits.

In a world of wide-ranging choice, people need categories. In an age of skepticism and media diversification, they need to easily understand who you are and how to relate to your ministry. Otherwise, you'll be lost in the sea of alternatives.

The *Wall Street Journal* reports that there are 500,000 Americans involved in launching their own company each year, and 10 percent to 15 percent of working adults are involved in some type of entrepreneurial activity.[2] There is a natural inclination in the United States to own our own business. Right now we're experiencing the most entrepreneurial period in our history. That energy has no doubt spilled over into religious and nonprofit activities as well. It doesn't take much searching to find a nonprofit foundation for nearly every disease or problem you can imagine, and in some cities, churches seem to sit on every street corner. Christian magazines are filled with advertisements for religious conferences, ministry outreaches, books and more.

Whatever good this abundance brings to the world, it also brings confusion and clutter for people trying to make sense of it all.

In my meeting, the ministry leader began to understand. "So how do audiences relate to people and ministries they see out there right now?"

I encouraged him to consider radio and TV ministries over the last 20 years or so. The most successful ministries may teach on a wide variety of issues, but in most cases, they each have an overarching theme to their life and ministry. Until he retired from pastoral ministry a few years ago, my own pastor was Jack Hayford at The Church On The Way in Van Nuys, California. As a pastor, Jack is a brilliant teacher and has spent decades preaching and teaching on an incredibly wide range of subjects in response to God's calling and the needs of the congregation. But in spite of that range and depth, I believe that Jack is motivated and driven by "worship." He is endlessly fascinated with the subject, both as a pastor and as a musician. As a result, he has taught today's Church volumes on the issue. Many would say he's the single greatest voice in the Christian community on the importance of godly worship in the church today.

Bottom line, if you cut Jack, he bleeds worship.

I rattled off a list of other names from the world of media ministry. Whether you agree with their theology or not, in most people's minds:

- Billy Graham is the *salvation* guy.
- Robert Schuller is the *motivation* guy.
- Benny Hinn is the *healing* guy.
- Ken Copeland is the *faith* guy.
- Larry Jones is the *feeding children* guy.
- Rod Parsley is the *Pentecostal* guy.
- James Dobson is the *family* guy.
- Don Colbert is the *health* guy.
- Joel Osteen is the *inspiration* guy.

And on the female side:

- Joyce Meyer is about *enjoying everyday life*.

Granted, that may be considered a crude way to look at it, but for millions of people, that's exactly how they view these ministry personalities.

In a world of choices, defining these ministries gives the audience an easy handle and allows them to have a quick understanding of who a particular pastor or ministry leader is and where his or her focus lies. Think of your brain as acting like a filter to help you sort through the growing flood of information that surrounds you every day.

Branding consultant Marty Neumeier calls today's culture information-rich and time-poor. In this environment, we need easy ways to help us get to the real information we need to make decisions about life.

To the viewer, supporter or church member, it's ultimately about a person, church or organization's identity helping people understand who they are and what they mean to a person's life.

It's about the story that surrounds who you are—a story that creates focus for your ministry.

In short, it's about your "brand."

I would ask you the same thing I asked that ministry leader in our creative meeting: *What do people think of when they think of you?*

A successful church, ministry or nonprofit organization happens at the intersection of a number of issues, not the least of which is calling, vision, ability, commitment, resources, exposure, location and education. There's no question that a pastor who can't preach will face obstacles, an evangelist with no calling will eventually collapse, and the leader of any nonprofit organization with no vision will never get very far.

But this book is about what happens when all those things fall into place and the spark *still* doesn't happen. When a church with all the right ingredients still struggles; when a gifted pastor never reaches a larger audience; or when a wonderful ministry can't seem to break through a particular barrier.

It could also happen to a church or ministry of any size that has been successful in the past, but like the pastor in my creative meeting, suddenly and with no explanation, the ministry stops getting results.

When that happens, it's not about what you do; it's about how you're perceived.

In a media-driven culture, when a church, ministry or nonprofit organization doesn't have a clear and compelling story that surrounds it, no amount of qualifications, resources, advertising or leadership can overcome the deficit. And it doesn't even matter if the organization experienced great success in the past. As James Twitchell in his book *Branded Nation* reminds us, "Observe the current state of the once-dominant Episcopal Church. Episcopalians committed an unforgivable marketing sin: they forgot their brand because they lost their story."[3]

> *I did everything they told me in seminary. I was a good preacher, had a committed ministry team, hired the right church-growth experts and fund-raisers, I prayed until my carpet wore through and I still never went beyond a local ministry. Was that God's plan for me? Possibly, but I couldn't help but wonder how the new media world has impacted our outreach, and if I was missing that connection.*
>
> **PASTOR IN THE MIDWEST**

Ideas Are Powerful, and Stories Are Ideas in Action

I hosted a 10-year anniversary event for a European nonprofit satellite TV network. The formal event was held in the Ronald Reagan Presidential Library in Simi Valley, California. Before the dinner, we were taken on a tour of the presidential museum, Ronald and Nancy's private quarters and even a tour of Air Force One, majestically enshrined in its own wing of the museum.

As we walked through the exhibits—particularly the areas chronicling President Reagan's role in the fall of the Soviet Union—I was captivated by a powerful inscription on the wall of the exhibit. It was a quote from Soviet leader Joseph Stalin:

> Ideas are more powerful than guns. We would not let our enemies have guns, why should we let them have ideas?

The quotation stands in clear testimony to the power of ideas and just how desperately the Soviet Union attempted to control those ideas. Today, that scenario is being played out as the government of Iran desperately studies how China has grown their economy while still controlling the political ideas of its population. They want the booming economy that innovation brings, while at the same time they want to control the ideas that make the innovation happen.

Just like the former Soviet Union, the leadership of Iran understands the explosive power of ideas.

This book isn't about public relations; it's about ideas. It's about using the power of storytelling to create a life-changing impression of you and your organization in the minds of your viewers, church members, partners, visitors and supporters. It's not about manipulation but about helping people clearly understand who you are and how you can impact their lives.

The media today is a digital cacophony of voices and images. To stand out in that ocean of choices takes more than excellent sermons, quality resources, professional programs and good intentions.

Connecting with a Culture that Changes at Light Speed

Shortly after the invasion of Afghanistan, I watched a national television news program broadcast a "discussion" (read: debate) about America's decision to invade that country in pursuit of terrorism. The discussion focused on religious leaders from various backgrounds, and it had the usual cast of characters:

- A successful New Age religious writer
- A liberal bishop from a major denomination
- A popular teacher of Eastern religion
- A well-known conservative pastor and radio preacher

As I listened to the interview, I first paid attention to the integrity of their arguments. The first three offered glib sound-bite responses to the questions. These particular men were intellectually shallow, and it didn't take long to see that they didn't have any real answers. Apparently, they had been chosen because of their media popularity rather than their academic or political insight. But when it came to their attitude and demeanor, I noticed they were warm and friendly. They looked the interviewer directly in the eye and were engaging and conversational.

The conservative pastor and radio preacher was actually far more eloquent and solid in his answers. He had a strong biblical response, was intellectually deep and made real sense. On the other hand, he was cold and unfriendly—almost arrogant. He refused to engage the others and instead appeared aloof and condescending.

At the end, I realized that although the conservative pastor had presented far better and more authoritative answers, in the eye of the viewers, he had lost the debate. I was so frustrated at the disconnect between his abilities and people's perception of him that I wrote him a letter. To my surprise, he wrote back.

His answer was less than satisfying. When I pointed out my opinion that he gave the best answers, but when it came to the public's perception, he lost the debate, his answer was essentially: *"I don't care. God didn't call me to be liked. After all, they liked Jesus, and they crucified Him. I'm called to speak the truth, and frankly, I don't care what people think."*

An earlier generation might have interpreted that response as bold and uncompromising. But I interpret it as being ignorant of the times in which we live.

> *When you persuade, speak of interest, not of reason.*
> **BENJAMIN FRANKLIN**

That pastor didn't have a clue about how to communicate in a media-driven culture. I would never question his answers in the discussion or even the intent of his heart, but I would argue with how his superior and arrogant attitude turned away many who might have been impacted by his remarks. People establish a gut-level connection with a person based on their values and perception long before they buy into the person's message.

That's what political consultants and writers Douglas B. Sosnick, Matthew J. Dowd and Ron Fournier discovered in the book *Applebee's America: How Successful Political, Business, and Religious Leaders Connect with the New American Culture*:

> Values are what Americans want to see in a candidate, corporation, or church before they're even willing to consider their policies and products. The choices people make about politics, consumer goods, and even religion are driven by emotions, rather than intellect.[4]

That's not a criticism of intellectual pursuit, and I wish more churches in America taught deeper doctrinal principles. But when a consumer makes the initial connection, it's not about *content;* it's about the *brand.* The values, story and sense of authenticity that surround a political candidate, business person or religious leader are far more important in that first moment.

There was a time when "packaging" had little impact on ministry, but not today. For a visually oriented, media-savvy generation, it's about more than just the message; it's also about the medium. And it's about the brand.

A Media-driven Culture Changes the Equation for Ministry

The apostle Paul lived out his ministry in the context of Roman domination; William Wilberforce campaigned in Parliament under the shadow of the British slave trade; Dietrich Bonhoeffer struggled under Nazi occupation. Today, we live in a media-dominated culture and must operate our churches, ministries or nonprofit organizations in that technological context.

In another age, all a preacher needed to be successful was a good Bible, a calling from God and strong lungs. In a digital culture, where a typical American deals with as many as 3,000 commercial messages a day, how does the voice of your church, ministry or nonprofit organization rise above the racket?

CHAPTER ONE

LIVING IN A MEDIA-DRIVEN CULTURE

Entertainment—not autos, not steel, not financial services—is fast becoming the driving wheel of the new world economy.
MICHAEL J. WOLF, *THE ENTERTAINMENT ECONOMY*[1]

I once heard it said that if an alien from another planet were to examine the United States and write an evaluation of our religious habits, he would probably conclude that Oprah is America's pastor, the vestments of the twenty-first-century church are manufactured by Nike, the communion table is poured by a barista from Starbucks, and in the children's department, a clown from McDonald's is certainly more widely recognized than Jesus of Nazareth. Today, people confess their sins on daytime television, purge their guilt by donating to TV evangelists, and seek redemption through the story arc in an action movie.

This information isn't anything new. At a typical religious conference today, people will debate the collapse of moral values, discuss the impact of living in an entertainment culture, or argue whether or not we should protest, boycott or engage.

Many blame the widening gap between the Church and state; others point to the growing permissiveness of society; and still others fault explicit sex and violence on television. No matter how you look at it, culture today is far more coarse, ragged and uncertain than it was a generation ago.

As people have since the beginning of time, when society feels uncertain, they look for spiritual answers. Religious belief comforts us during times of difficulty. It provides a moral bearing and imparts meaning and purpose that materialism simply can't provide.

During the last few years, there has been a trend in advertising and marketing to explore the connections between religion and branding. As advertisers search for more and more effective ways to connect products with consumers, they've stumbled upon the power of "meaning." If you can link a product to a consumer's personal identity, the connection becomes far stronger and the relationship sticks for a much longer period of time.

That's no surprise to the Church, which has known its impact for thousands of years. The Bible itself says, "Train up a child in the way he should go, and when he is old, he will not depart from it" (Prov. 22:6). As a young preacher's kid growing up in the South, I heard my father preach that if you could get young people into church as children, the chances were far higher that they would continue that relationship for the rest of their lives.

Today, cell phone companies, fashion designers, food producers, television networks, and more, focus specifically on children in order to make them brand conscious for life. We call them "early adopters."

A Brand Stays Forever

Branding is about identity. Even in the nuclear age, there isn't a more powerful force on the earth. "Identity politics" is changing the political scene, as gays, feminists and ethnic groups all want a place at the table. Wars are fought over cultural identity, and seemingly normal people commit horrific crimes simply to save face. As I write this, a highly regarded female astronaut has just driven at high speed from Texas to Florida, allegedly wearing a diaper so that she wouldn't have to make a restroom stop—all to confront a woman she believed was competing for her boyfriend. When she was arrested, the police found kidnapping tools, such as rope and duct tape, in her car. Her career is over, she has been humiliated in the press, and years of study, training and preparation have gone down the drain—all because of jealousy and the embarrassment of potentially losing her astronaut boyfriend to another woman.

In Los Angeles, gang members are willing to die for other members, even though they barely know them. Gang identity on the streets is so strong that few things—sometimes not even family ties—can break that hold.

Who we are is an issue of identity, integrity and purpose, and we're willing to go to great lengths to keep that identity unique and strong.

> *The faster globalism removes barriers, the faster people erect new ones. They create intimate worlds they can understand, and where they can be somebody and feel as if they belong. They create tribes.*
>
> **MARTY NEUMEISTER, *THE BRAND GAP*** [2]

It's natural that marketers should look to religion for inspiration. Religion is all about identity. *Who am I? Why am I here? What's my purpose in life?* Besides the Bible, Pastor Rick Warren's book *The Purpose Driven Life* has become one of the bestselling books of all time, because it touched a nerve about the most important question of our lives: How do I discover my purpose?

In future chapters, we'll discuss many of the current thinkers who have made the connection between branding and religion; but for the most part, they are looking from the outside in. For my purposes, I'm more interested in examining the question from the opposite direction. As I said, I'm a preacher's kid who grew up in the church during turbulent times in its history. During the fifties and sixties, the church was struggling for its identity amid the "death of God" theologians, the creeping liberalism of the Church and the ongoing culture wars. During that time, the Church changed dramatically as evangelicalism grew, Charismatic and Pentecostal churches exploded, and we experienced a major shift in church growth. Historic mainline denominations took sides on the issue of the "social gospel," and pastors debated the role of the supernatural and the legitimacy of Christ's miracles.

Out of that, a church emerged, populated by a younger generation that understood the power of media, that was not content with what they perceived as propaganda and that searched for new methods to share an eternal message.

Having experienced those changes on the front lines of ministry, I became one of the new breed of believers in America. Rather than pursue my father's calling as a pastor, I finished a bachelor's degree in television and film studies, a master's in journalism, and a Ph.D. in theology. It took awhile, but my goal was to merge the historic Christian faith with more effective methods of sharing that story in a media-driven culture. Since that time, I've produced programs in more than 40 countries around the world, split my work between secular and religious programming, and consulted on media issues for some of the largest and most effective churches and nonprofit organizations in the world.

My goal was simple: How do we share a life-changing message with a culture that has lost interest? How can our message compete with the cacophony of voices in the media? How have churches and religious organizations become so irrelevant? Why is religious media so out of touch with the culture? If we are actually speaking truth with a capital *T*, why isn't anyone listening?

As a result, it wasn't long before I realized that when it came to actually impacting the culture, the Church has a huge problem:

We've lost our story.

From the earliest days of Hebrew storytellers sitting around campfires in the deserts of the Middle East, storytelling has been the core of every culture known to man.

From the parables of Jesus to the medieval mystery and passion plays, from the rise of the modern novel to motion pictures and television, storytelling has transcended government, culture and philosophy.

Every great civilization has creation stories and tales of great exploits that define their moral universe. *The Odyssey, The Iliad, The Bible, Beowulf* and *The Mahabharata* are seminal stories that identify the personalities of various cultures and define their reason for being. The way stories are told has changed over the centuries, but the stories themselves have not lost their meaning or importance in people's lives.

There is no question that today the media has added an explosive element to the story. The statistics are unrelenting:

- 99 percent of households in America have at least one television.
- 66 percent have three or more sets.
- The average household has the television on 6 hours and 47 minutes per day.
- 70 percent of day-care centers use television in a typical day.
- By the time a child finishes elementary school, he has seen 8,000 murders on television.

- By age 18, he has seen more than 200,000 violent acts.
- 66 percent of Americans watch TV while they eat dinner.[3]

As a result, the average family only spends 3.5 minutes per week in meaningful conversation with their children.[4]

And that's just television.

I find television very educating. Every time somebody turns on the set, I go into the other room and read a book.

COMEDIAN GROUCHO MARX

Today, more and more media platforms are competing with television for priority in our lives. Personal computers, digital music players, email, instant messaging, cell phones, and more, are slicing up our lives into digital compartments, and their power has become frightening.

The *Los Angeles Times* reported on a study that indicated one-third of Korean high school students make as many as 90 cell phone calls per day.[5] The study also linked high cell phone use to rates of depression.

For those of you who slept through the revolution, today eBay has 168 million users worldwide; MySpace.com, by 2006, had registered 100 million users; there are 50 million blogs; and 10 million people use CraigsList to search for classifieds. By the time you read this book, those numbers will be significantly higher.

When my daughters were in middle school, they could design their own websites. As a result, young people today value their digital space more than their people space. In other words, they'd rather spend time *online* with friends than actually *face to face* with friends. As a result, *the search for meaning* has been replaced by the search for *the next big thing*.

In this media-driven environment, influence has shifted from the power of church and community to the power of corporate brands, and they wield enormous power.

According to James Twitchell, professor of English and advertising at the University of Florida:

> Much of our shared knowledge about ourselves and our culture comes to us through a commercial process of storytelling called "branding." The process starts early. A marketing professor estimates that 10 percent of a two-year-old's nouns are brand names. And an English study estimates that one out of every four babies speaks a brand name as a first word.[6]

This book isn't about the horrors of media, advertising or entertainment. There are plenty of books, scholarly journals and research out there that will make your hair stand on end when it comes to that subject. Does media violence begat real violence? Is the media responsible for the dumbing down of America? Has visual literacy displaced reading skills in schools? The questions go on and on, and by one count, more than 4,000 studies have been completed just on the effects of TV on children alone.

This book takes a different approach. The fact is that we're immersed in a media-driven culture. Our alarm goes off in the morning playing music from our favorite radio station; we get up and turn on the morning news to see what's happening in the world. We read the paper over breakfast. We listen to the car radio, music CD or a podcast on the way to work. We spend the day at our desk working by computer, periodically checking our email or stock prices on our PDA. We listen to the radio on the way home. We watch the evening news over dinner. We catch our favorite TV programs in prime time, then take a last peek at our email or check in online at eBay. Then we watch the "eyewitness news" right before we hit the sack, and maybe a few minutes of a popular late-night talk show.

Nearly every waking moment of our life intersects with the media in some way. And although that much exposure can't be a good thing, the momentum is strong. So while we can't stop it, we at least need to understand it.

When I was in college in the early seventies, studying media, I read Jerry Mander's classic book, *Four Arguments for the Elimination of Television*. It was a fascinating book that was difficult to argue with. But its central premise—that we should completely eliminate television—was something that even then I realized was never going to happen.

Since that time, thousands of studies have appeared linking violence, anti-social behavior, depression, lack of community, and more, to media use; but the truth is, we still watch the big game, we still check our email, and if you're so inclined, you can still find plenty of preachers on television.

I've been a producer and director for more than 30 years, most of that time in Hollywood. I own a production and consulting company that works with some of the largest and most effective churches and ministries in the country, helping them use media to make an impact in the culture. I'm also a founding partner in a secular television commercial company that produces spots for some of the largest companies in America. So I have a foot in both worlds—Christian media and secular media. Over the years, I've learned how to navigate our clients through the media minefields from both sides of the fence.

More Than Just a Connection

I speak the language of Christianity, and I also speak the language of media. I don't believe there's simply a connection between branding and religion; I believe that religious experience is what the core of branding is all about.

As someone who has spent a lifetime sharing his faith with others, I have something to say about the influence that faith has on issues of personal identity, value and the search for meaning. Whether you're a nonbeliever investigating information on how to use branding to make your product connect more deeply with a customer, or you're a believer wondering how to expose your church or ministry to a greater audience, this book will provide real answers.

The New Media World

Television was once called a vast wasteland, and it's hard to argue with that description. Even today, with multiple cable and satellite channels, religious and family channels and other positive signs, there is still a lot of desert out there in the media landscape.

But recently, the mass media has changed in a way that no one expected. In fact, I predict that our lifetime will be remembered as the era when mass media died. The truth is, it has been murdered. The suspects include digital music and video players, broadband Internet connections, blogging, and online entertainment.

Today media is about personalization. The mass audience isn't interested in the same thing anymore. And they want their media customized. On my digital music player, I have classic rock and roll, bluegrass, praise and worship, Frank Sinatra, Southern gospel and even opera. I'm not interested in what radio stations *think* I need, because now I can customize my own play list.

So what does this mean for those of us interested in sharing our faith or selling products through the media?

It means that it's time to wake up to the change.

In the church, pastors, Christian leaders and broadcasters always thought they had the answers to what their audience wanted and, more important, the audience would listen. Today the audience is in charge. In a virtually unlimited channel universe, the audience has more choices than ever before, and for us to justify their attention, we need to get on their wavelength.

After all, it doesn't matter if you have a great message if no one is listening.

The twenty-first century is changing everything about how to get your message to an audience. Yesterday it was about dumping the same message on the mass audience because they didn't have much choice. Today it's about making a connection—the kind of connection that not only makes them want to hear what you have to say but also makes them respond.

Understanding that connection is a critical step in finding your audience.

CHAPTER TWO

THE INFLUENCE OF A COMPELLING BRAND

If the business were split up, I would take the brands, trademarks, and goodwill, and you could have all the bricks and mortar—and I would do better than you.

JOHN STUART, FORMER CHAIRMAN OF QUAKER OATS CORPORATION

"Branding" could be the single most misunderstood term in all of American business. As a result, churches and ministries have mistakenly applied its principles in a variety of disastrous ways, and many end up thinking that branding is something born in the bowels of hell.

A visit to the business book section of a local bookstore will reveal an amazing number of titles: *Brand Leadership, Building Strong Brands, A Brand New World, Branded Nation, Brand Warfare, Strategic Brand Management, Be Your Own Brand, The 22 Immutable Laws of Branding, Brand Asset Management, Managing Brand Equity,* and many more. That tidal wave of branding volumes causes many executives to look to branding as a magic bullet that will solve all their marketing headaches.

There's no question that branding has made a deep impact on the culture. In a world where Ronald McDonald is the most recognized man in America and the golden arches are more familiar than the Red Cross; where highway billboards display a Nike swoosh with no text or pictures, and one of the most popular computer navigation programs in Hollywood is the "global Starbucks locator," something is definitely up.

But what exactly is branding?

At its core, branding is simply the art of surrounding a product, organization or person with a powerful and compelling story. Just as you can brand a product like Nike or Starbucks, you can also brand organizations like churches, nonprofit groups and even individuals. Oprah probably has the most widely recognized personal brand in America, and she's very careful about controlling her look, style and the public's perception. I recently did a television commercial, and we wanted to use some still photographs of Oprah. I discovered just how difficult it was to get permission to use her image. She understands the power of a compelling brand and has become very astute at controlling every aspect of how she is perceived.

But how did this come about? How did the "story" about a product become more important than the product itself?

It's all about competition and the need to distinguish the product from the rest of the pack. At its most basic level, branding provides answers to the simple human need to differentiate one thing from another. Our present concept of branding came from cattle drives and the need to brand cows to maintain ownership. Things haven't changed that much from the time of pressing red-hot iron into the flesh of herds of cattle, to monogramming a little horse and rider on a Ralph Lauren dress shirt (worn by herds of businessmen).

Before the industrial revolution in this country, there was pretty much one brand of soap, one type of sugar, one kind of bread. It was a simple world back then, but it was also a world without variety. In those days, most products were handmade, and the first to the market usually won the day.

As a result, life was defined by social class, nationality, race, politics, religion or the essential needs of life, such as food, clothing, shelter and sex.

The industrial revolution gave inventors and business leaders the ability to create a massive surplus. It also paved the way for more competition, as more and more companies were able to create their own versions of products.

As a result, our lives burst out of the classifications and identities we had held for centuries and changed their focus to the wide variety of products hitting the shelves. Thus, for the first time, you could be known for the car you drove, the brand of suit you wore, the perfume you used or the games you played. As the consumer culture caught hold, we could identify ourselves with a virtually unlimited range of goods and services to the point that today we proudly wear Armani suits, carry a Prada handbag, wear a Rolex watch, drive a Lexus or drink Starbucks coffee.

My wife, Kathleen, and I recently attended a wedding in Palm Springs, California. What we didn't realize was that the wedding was scheduled the same weekend as a motorcycle rally that brought 30,000 bikers to the streets of this desert city.

Watching the thousands of bikers that weekend, I was reminded of the tremendous power of the Harley-Davidson brand. "Harleys" were easily the overwhelming choice among the bikers, but loyalty to their beloved brand didn't stop with the motorcycles. They also sported Harley-Davidson leather jackets, helmets, hats, headscarves, gloves, saddlebags, T-shirts, chaps, and more. Stores featured Harley-Davidson children's clothes and women's lingerie.

Talking to a few of the bikers, I realized that the ultimate conceit is how they consider themselves "outsiders," "rebels" and "independents." Some told me they felt they were the last real outlaws and freethinkers left on the planet. They weren't loyal to anything but themselves, and they relished the kind of freedom they felt people like me couldn't possibly enjoy.

But as they enthusiastically shared with me about how independent they felt, they were sitting on a Harley-Davidson motorcycle and wearing all the branded clothes that came with it. I tried my best, but with one biker I couldn't find a single item of clothing he wore that didn't have the company logo on it somewhere.

In truth, while they imagined themselves as rebels, they were actually committed worshipers at the altar of Harley-Davidson.

> *Simply because in a world that is bewildering in terms of competitive clamor, in which rational choice has become almost impossible, brands represent clarity, reassurance, consistency, status, membership–everything that enables human beings to help define themselves. Brands represent identity.*
>
> **WALLY OLINS, CHAIRMAN OF SAFFRON BRAND CONSULTANTS**

In a nonprofit or religious environment, the process isn't much different. You may be a pastor wanting to make a more significant impression in your community, a media ministry reaching out to a larger support base, a missions organization attempting to raise funding, or a museum trying to raise your profile in a geographic region. Whatever the purpose, the goal is to win the hearts and minds of the largest audience possible and imprint an indelible story around your church, ministry or mission.

The power of these stories and the hold they exert over our lives is remarkable, and many would say the power of story is embedded in our genetic makeup. From the ancient days of the Israelite storytellers who recited the epic chronicles of Abraham, Isaac and Jacob, to the writers, preachers and filmmakers of today, we are a story-driven people, and we use stories to make sense of life.

It's no surprise that the most watched television programs year after year are situation comedies, episodic dramas and movies—all story-driven formats. Even reality programming needs a story to drive the momentum forward. Whether it's danger, family tension or competition, the stories captured in reality television simply continue an ancient tradition (perhaps with a little more tossed in as well).

Stories work because we want to experience the emotions, feelings and passions of others who have encountered the challenges we face each day. We love to see a hero prevail, bad guys get their due, or weep with a tragic loss.

In 1954, the year of my birth, TV dinners, I Love Lucy *and the H-Bomb were invented, and to this day, I'm not sure if there was a connection.*

The year I was born, Decca Records recorded rock 'n' roll's first real smash hit, "Shake, Rattle and Roll"; Elvis Presley made his first record; and Walt Disney went on television. TV was exploding, and Walt Disney was one of the first to realize the magnetic power of a compelling brand.

When the *Davy Crockett* program debuted on national television, I had to have a coonskin cap, a pioneer rifle and the leather outfit that completed the look. I had a Davy Crockett lunchbox, T-shirt, pencil and belt, and I was ready for attacks from Indians, raging bears or my little sister. My mother had to force me to take off my coonskin cap at bedtime or I would have worn it 24/7.

I wanted to be Davy Crockett, and even though I was a young child, I adopted his story as my own.

Eventually, I did the same with Superman, Batman, The Green Hornet, James Bond, and others. All because I loved the stories.

I saw my two daughters do the same thing with all the Disney princesses. Both of my daughters had Snow White dresses, and they literally wore them until they disintegrated. Long after they had become rags, those dresses were still our daughters' favorites. My girls were hypnotized by the story of the princess who was cast out, who never gave up and eventually found her prince.

Stories have remarkable power, which is exactly the reason Jesus used them.

Jesus told stories during His three years of adult ministry on the earth. During that short time, He had to teach a message that wouldn't simply change people's lives during His lifetime, but transform the world for ages to come. If you had faced that challenge, what would you have done?

Most pastors I know would start with a mission statement. Then they would outline their doctrinal principles and statement of faith. Then they would find a building, preferably one with good parking and the ability to expand. Then, realizing the need to leave a legacy in the faith, they would start working on their theology and perhaps throw in a handful of leadership principles and church-growth tips. Then they'd be ready.

But it's worth asking the question on the famous bracelets: WWJD? (What would Jesus do?)

Jesus did what many pastors in that position would probably consider a real career killer. He started telling stories. And He told stories that He didn't even explain. Sometimes He would enlighten the disciples in private, but rarely did He say the words in public, "Now let me tell you what that means."

Plus, the stories weren't that profound. They didn't involve kings or princes, wars or major conflict, and they certainly weren't particularly deep. All the wonderful elements that make great legends were left out. There weren't even any epic tales of heroes and damsels in distress.

Most of Jesus' stories were just everyday people doing everyday things. They weren't particularly exciting, romantic or even thrilling.

Why? Why was Jesus ready to risk only three years of ministry by telling simple stories?

Morpheus said it best in the movie The Matrix. *He described it as a "splinter in your mind."*

Stories drill deeply into your brain and explode later with meaning. Sometimes the meaning comes when you least expect it. Stories impact audiences because each person interprets the story in light of his or her own personal situation. As a result, the impact is far greater than a simple object lesson or teaching session.

I'm reminded of the power of the *Andy Griffith Show*, possibly the greatest comedy series ever filmed. Andy could disarm any situation by simply telling a story.

In many cases, you can interchangeably use the words "brand," "story" and "reputation." Branding is about building trust and loyalty and extending your customer relationships far beyond a single transaction.

My father was a pastor who owned a 7,000-volume library. He was also a historian, and along with a vast number of books on theology and Christian studies, many of those volumes were about the Civil War and World War II. My father hit the beach with the First Marine Division in the Pacific at Guadalcanal, and his unit slugged their way through heavy enemy fire and tremendous losses to take the island for the Allies. It was a key wartime position for an airfield, and although it was a bloody campaign, it was to become a critical staging point against the Japanese.

Like most men who fought in World War II, the memory has remained remarkably vivid throughout his life. As a result, he built a massive collection of books on the Pacific campaign. He was born into a mill family that for generations had labored folding sheets and towels, or worked their fingers to the bone at looms in colossal North Carolina cotton mills. But the war broke that cycle and gave my father a way out. As quickly as he could, he grabbed the opportunity, enlisted and never looked back. After the war, he attended college and, eventually, graduate school. As a pastor, he had four master's degrees and two doctorates. Education was my father's way out of poverty. He taught me that learning was incredibly valuable.

But among those 7,000 books in his collection, my father never owned a single novel.

He believed that if it wasn't "true" it was a waste of time. As a result, I never understood the power of fiction until I attended college myself. That was when I discovered that stories might not be true but that they express truth with a capital *T*. Stories help us define who we are, where we came from and where we're going. Stories are like a compass to help us find our bearings, and they provide a place of belonging.

That's why stories have become the central focus of the art of branding; and that's how branding has become a religion for a new generation.

Chapter Three

THE POWER OF BRAND PERCEPTION

(Why It's Just as Important as Reality)

Science is nothing but perception.
PLATO

It is the function of art to renew our perception. What we are familiar with we cease to see. The writer shakes up the familiar scene, and, as if by magic, we see a new meaning in it.
ANAÏS NIN, AVANT-GARDE NOVELIST

The key to effective branding is that a successful brand isn't what *you* say it is; it's what *they* say it is. For instance, it doesn't matter if the local food bank is the best in the nation if word leaks out that it's giving away tainted produce. It won't matter that you're a brilliant pastor if your congregation thinks you're a hack. And it certainly won't matter that a humanitarian organization is global if nobody's ever heard of it.

In other words, it's about *perception*.

Telling an effective story about your church, ministry, project or yourself begins with understanding the power of perception. In a media-driven culture, perception can be even more important than reality because, with the advent of technology, word travels fast. Whether it's a simple email message that is continually forwarded exponentially to everyone in your address book, a viral video that's distributed though the Web, or the convenience of cell phones, in the digital age, it's tough to keep a lid on bad news, as various American presidents have discovered with White House leaks.

I often tell about my first real experience with understanding the power of perception. I was in my early twenties and had the opportunity to lead a film crew to the headwaters of the Amazon River in Brazil to film the work of a medical relief team. It was an exciting opportunity, but I had no idea of the challenge I would face trying to get our film equipment through customs in the Brazilian city of Manaus. The city is located about 1,000 miles upriver from the Atlantic, and today is a beautiful city of nearly 2 million people. When we arrived at the airport, which had been literally carved out of the jungle, I had a three-man crew and a number of large cases of film equipment that had to be cleared through customs.

I've filmed in about 40 countries around the world. I have survived military coups in Africa, been chased by Communist sympathizers in the Caribbean, lived with Nomads in the deserts of the Middle East, bribed corrupt customs officials to release equipment (and sometimes my people), and a host of other strange and sometimes dangerous situations, but I was not ready for the unusual response I received from one particular customs official as we were trying to get into Brazil.

"Can you prove you're a filmmaker from the United States?" he asked.

I had my passport, customs documentation and equipment lists, but I've never actually been asked to prove what I do for a living. After all, it's not like we carry a membership card or diploma around to prove we're in some type of "filmmaker's club."

"Well, I'm sorry, Mr. Cooke. Until you can prove to me you're actually an official filmmaker from the United States, I can't allow your equipment into the country. You're welcome to come in, but I'll have to keep your equipment locked here in customs until you can provide adequate documentation."

Official filmmaker?! It was insane. It's not as if tourists carry nearly a million dollars worth of film and video equipment on vacation. We argued and argued, but nothing worked. So I took the crew to the hotel, frustrated and upset, because we still had airplane flights, boat charters and numerous other connections to meet; and now everything was being thrown into chaos. We paced the hotel room, tried to make phone calls and discussed every possible solution, but came up empty.

The jungle heat and humidity didn't help. Every day we would travel back to the customs official and request the equipment, and every day he would turn us down. Quietly, we even offered him a bribe, since that technique had worked in plenty of other places, but no dice, he was an honest guy and he just wouldn't budge.

After a few days, we considered returning to the United States in failure, knowing that we had wasted thousands of dollars to get this far, with nothing to show for it.

The problem was perception.

No matter how many passports, equipment lists and travel arrangements I showed the customs official, for some reason he was convinced that we weren't actual filmmakers. We argued until we were exhausted, but his *perception* just wouldn't change.

Finally, after four days of haggling and arguing, I walked slowly back to my room knowing that we had tried everything and still failed. When I started to undress for the night, I pulled my wallet out of my jeans pocket and for some reason decided to flip through the back section where I kept my insurance cards and driver's license, and that's when the card that changed everything fell out.

Years before, a nonprofit organization in Hollywood began publishing a magazine devoted to filmmaking, called *American Film*. It was a wonderful magazine for anyone who truly loved movies, because it wasn't a trendy publication about movie stars. It featured real articles about the behind-the-scenes process of making films and included intimate interviews, interesting stories and other information about the industry. The magazine was a highly respected division of an organization still in existence today called the American Film Institute, which conducts classes and workshops for serious filmmakers and even sponsors major industry events.

At that time, when you signed up for a subscription to the magazine, you received a membership card into the American Film Institute. It didn't really mean anything more than the magazine subscription, except that it might get you into an occasional film screening or movie premiere.

When the American Film Institute magazine subscription card fell out of my wallet, it gave me a brilliant idea. The next morning, we were back in the customs official's office.

"You want proof that we are filmmakers from the United States, right?"

"That's correct," he replied, "and so far, I've seen nothing."

I whipped out my AFI card. Fortunately, the information on the card about the magazine subscription was printed on the back in very small letters, and I hoped he wouldn't notice too closely.

"I'm a member of the American Film Institute." I pointed at the front. "There, you can see my name printed on my membership card."

The customs official looked at the card carefully, compared the signature with my passport, and then a light switched on in his head. His demeanor changed, and suddenly, he jumped to his feet, grinning like a car salesman who has just made a deal.

"Why didn't you tell me you were a member of the American Film Institute?" He beamed with excitement, as if he'd stumbled on a real celebrity. He had no idea what the AFI was, but it sure sounded impressive.

"Welcome to our country! Please enjoy your filming!"

He walked around the desk, embraced everyone on my crew and then led us into the warehouse where customs was holding our equipment. He couldn't have been nicer. The next thing we knew we were given a police escort with full sirens and lights back to the hotel, with government employees personally carrying our equipment and unloading it for us.

I kissed my AFI membership card, carefully tucked it away in my wallet and carried it faithfully for years, even after the actual magazine ceased publication. The simple magazine subscription card meant nothing in itself, but it completely changed the perception of that customs official. When his perception changed, we went from being tourists at best (and con artists at worst) to being celebrated filmmakers from the United States, deserving official government approval and support.

In more than 25 years of active work in the entertainment industry, I've seen few situations where perception played such an important role.

The influence of the mass media in our culture is changing everything, and "perception" is the language spoken by modern media. In a world where sound bites heavily influence the political process, the unique characteristics of mass media now affect every aspect of our lives. Public relations has become an art form as companies and organizations (and even celebrities) confront the need to impact and hopefully control public opinion. Perception has become a critical part of advertising campaigns, press releases and public statements.

As a commercial director and media consultant in Hollywood, *perception* is my business. I deal in the visual world of products and people and how they are perceived by the viewing audience. Today, in a media-saturated culture, perception is the currency of commerce.

It's not about facts; it's about perception.

As a person of faith in the industry, I've spent years wrestling with the moral implications of perception. Watching tobacco companies position cigarettes as non-addictive, casino owners position themselves as family entertainment, and pornographers position themselves as champions of free speech, I looked at the art of perception as a negative, deceitful proposition.

Indeed it can be, but like many things, I learned that it also has a flip side as I began to study how Jesus went to great lengths to impact the public perception of His ministry and His purpose on the earth.

Was Jesus a Brand Manager?

Jesus came to Earth in a different way than people expected. They wanted a king; He was born into poverty.

He preached a different message than people expected. They wanted a revolution; He preached a message of love.

When one of His best friends was dying, against the wishes of His friends, Jesus took His time getting to Lazarus.

He healed a man, and then told him not to tell anyone.

He carefully chose the men who would be His closest associates.

During the height of His popularity, He withdrew to remote places to be alone.

He chose the method of His triumphal entry into Jerusalem.

When He could have escaped in the garden, He told Peter to stop fighting, and quietly allowed Himself to be arrested.

During the events that led to His execution, He even controlled the interrogation by Pilate by only responding to certain questions.

Jesus had a purpose and plan for His life, and He refused to let others determine His destiny or how He would be perceived.

Someone once said that if you don't control your perception, you'll live the rest of your life at the mercy of others who will. Who will write the story of your life? Will you leave your own legacy, or wait for others to create it for you?

Celebrity Culture

The global fascination with celebrities has been an important element in the realization of how important perception is today. For instance, with the advent of the relatively recent concept of "celebrity," the basis of fame has undergone a striking change.

In the past, a person became famous for accomplishing a significant task, such as making a great discovery, winning the championship football game or finding the cure for a deadly disease. But today, just being in the news makes someone famous, and actual accomplishment really isn't necessary anymore. A movie star showing up at a party makes front-page news, high-profile sexual affairs propel some to national TV interviews and book deals, and paparazzi photographers have made celebrity "journalism" the foundation of entire magazines.

If you have any idea what Paris Hilton actually does for a living, please let me know. She has no job and has never accomplished anything of significance, and yet she's the focus of celebrity journalism night after night in Hollywood. Featured at major industry parties, she's a sought-after guest (and is paid a fortune just to show up at those parties) because of her ability to attract attention.

Advertising Has Changed

That's also an interesting aspect of why the advertising industry has moved from "informational" advertising to "emotional" advertising. Since the beginning of modern media, the primary goal of marketers was to tell the public about the wonderful features of a product—how it works, the quality of the construction or the helpful features. But today, advertisers don't tell us *about* the product; they tell us *how we're going to feel* when we use the product. When was the last time you saw an athletic shoe commercial that described the high-quality materials that went into the shoes, the excellent construction or the useful features? Today, they're more interested in convincing you that when you strap on these shoes, you'll suddenly leap like an all-star, win championship sports events or fit in with a cooler crowd.

In the same way, beer advertising tells you very little about the distinguishing qualities of a particular brand or the high-level ingredients that went into the process. Instead they show you how that brand of beer will make you look and feel cool. You'll meet beautiful women at great parties and suddenly become more desirable and attractive to the opposite sex. It happens in nearly any product area you care to choose.

It's not about facts anymore; it's about perception.

One of the greatest challenges in the movie business is trying to control the perception of a particular movie. The massive studio machine that creates movie posters, trailers, TV spots and more is all about attempting to direct perceptions. When that machine fails, more than a hundred million dollars could be lost in the process. Is this movie a suspense thriller, a romantic comedy, or a horror film? Is it starring a popular actor? Is it directed at a certain age group? If the answers to these important questions are not provided by the advertising campaign that precedes the movie release, the movie may miss the very audience it's designed to reach. The history of Hollywood is littered with excellent films that simply missed their audience.

On the flip side, similar techniques are used to make a troubled film look better. No screenings for critics, stars who usually don't do interviews stumping for the film, or heightened budgets for advertising and promotion can all be signs that the studio is trying their best to cover up a potential flop.

Perception drives American business, retail products and even the government. When an American president lands a high-tech fighter plane on an aircraft carrier in the Pacific, wearing full pilot regalia and rallying the troops in front of a giant banner reading "Mission Accomplished," it's a victory of perception. He could have easily waited until the ship arrived in the harbor and addressed the soldiers from the dock in the comfort of his favorite suit; but the impact of landing a screaming fighter jet on the deck of an active warship heightens the perception of the event in the eyes of the public and causes his approval ratings to soar.

Like it or not, it's a brilliant move, even if it generates criticism later.

So how can we harness the power of perception?

Who You Are Is Important, but How You're Perceived Is Critical

In today's media-saturated culture, who you are becomes less important than how you're perceived. When researchers study the process of communication, they realize that the message being sent is not always the message being received. For a variety of reasons, few communicated messages actually arrive with the same intentions, information and impact.

If you're married, you know the drill—probably far too well.

For example, I heard a comedian describe that it took him years of marriage to unravel the real meaning of the word "tone."

He said, "I can talk all day at the office giving instructions, running meetings, making decisions, but when I walk in the door at home and use that same style voice, my wife says, 'Hey, don't use that tone with me.'"

The comedian said he always thought "tone" had to do with musical instruments—flat, sharp, harsh, soft. But to his wife, tone had more to do with attitude, and she wanted him to speak to her with a different attitude than he spoke with employees.

What was that again? It took him years to figure it out.

"I don't like that tone."

"Don't take that tone when you speak to me."

"Maybe you should take that tone right back to the office."

In my own marriage, we've experienced similar communication challenges, and some took me years to understand. How many men have made the mistake of answering truthfully the question, "Honey, does this dress make me look fat?" or "Do I look old in this?"

Truth is a wonderful thing, but sometimes it's better to run screaming from the room.

Hollywood spends millions to control perception.

From the earliest days of the movie industry, the major studios created vast machines to control the perception of their movie stars and the movies they produced. In fact, back in those days, it was not unusual for major studios to have local government officials, members of the press or police officers on a secret payroll so that they could quietly control the impact of potentially high-profile scandals. If movie stars who were featured in family friendly movies were caught committing adultery, being drunk and disorderly, or doing a criminal act, the studios could call in favors from elected officials or the press to keep a lid on the news.

Today, public morals and behavior have changed so much that it almost seems like the studios encourage rowdy behavior, but you can be sure that whatever image they want to create for a particular star is still carefully guarded and controlled—even if the questionable methods of an older era have been largely relinquished. In fact, the entertainment industry has given rise to the professional "publicist"someone whose job it is to help direct and control the public's perception of a movie, a TV series or star.

Few celebrities can be found without a hired publicist nearby. Stars want to be seen in the trendiest magazines, the hottest TV talk shows and the coolest Hollywood parties. A good publicist can make that happen. When you pick up a magazine with exclusive photos of celebrities attending important events, this didn't happen by chance. It was a long and sometimes complicated dance whose purpose was to make sure that a celebrity was seen in the right place, wore the right outfit from the hottest designer, hobnobbed with the beautiful people and ended up in just the right photograph to document the event for a national magazine or TV audience.

The Steven Spielberg movie *Catch Me If You Can* is a dramatic example of the power of perception in action. In the true story, young Frank Abagnale, Jr., was just a teenager, but he cashed millions of dollars in bad checks and passed himself off as a doctor, airline pilot, attorney and other personas for years, simply through the power of perception. He looked the part, talked the part and showed confidence and poise, so people just assumed that what he said must be true. He positioned himself in their minds in a certain way, and without the required skills for the job, it still worked even in different cultures around the world.

But perception is not just a matter of cheating people, and it's more than simply saving the reputation of careless actors or diverting public attention from serious criminal acts or public-relations problems.

The art of perception can also be used to promote positive projects, people, values or ideas.

For instance, major business leaders are getting into the picture and hiring publicists because they've discovered that influencing perception not only works with companies and products, but it also works with people. In today's environment of celebrity, CEOs around the country know that being seen in the right places can help them meet the right people, be perceived as major players and open doors for new strategic opportunities.

A number of years ago, the American public finally began to take the dangers of cigarette smoking seriously. For decades, research (even from tobacco companies) had indicated that cigarettes were a health hazard. Over the years, millions of people had died tragic deaths, but increasing numbers of young people were still taking up the habit, and those in authority soon realized that it would take more than facts to make a difference. It would also take a dramatic change in perception for people to finally act. When the government began researching the issue, they soon realized that one of the first steps for a successful effort had to be a change in the way the public perceived the problem.

That's when a series of massive advertising campaigns were born. These campaigns were designed to change our attitudes from thinking that smoking is glamorous and sexy to the reality that it is a nasty, disgusting killer. I'll never forget the power of the famous TV commercial featuring the interview with the woman who had survived cancer surgery, but in the process, doctors were forced to remove part of her tongue and throat. In spite of that horrifying result, she still chose to smoke through the ragged hole cut into her neck. I have no doubt that thousands of people quit smoking after being confronted with the dramatic and terrifying reality that particular commercial presented.

One of the greatest challenges the anti-smoking forces faced was the way that cigarettes were portrayed in the movies. For decades, smoking had been associated with exciting and glamorous movie characters. Find a good-looking movie hero, and chances were, he had a cigarette in his mouth. Sexy actresses? In between their provocative stares, they put a cigarette to their lips. Generations of young people had grown up with the perception that cigarette smoking was a vital part of living the good life and enjoying big-time success.

So pressure was put on Hollywood studios to change that perception by eliminating smoking from movies entirely—or at the very least, to rewrite scripts so that the act of smoking didn't appear in such a positive light. From that point on, cigarette smoking was discouraged, or in some cases, smoking was left to criminals, weirdos or other negative characters.

"Perception" is a powerful word and has enormous consequences.

It had an impact on perception about smoking. Of course, perception didn't change overnight, and even today we see occasional surges in on-screen smoking; but once the perception was changed, it dealt a major blow to the number of young people taking up the habit.

How can we use perception in our church, ministry or nonprofit organization? To what extent can we control the way the culture perceives us, and how can we use those techniques to make change happen and accomplish our goals? First, we need to understand that perception can be a positive tool.

The Positive Side of Perception

Too many religious believers view the perception issue as a negative tool of manipulation and refuse to consider its positive potential. They've seen the way that some alcohol advertisers have attempted to influence teens to drink, or the way some cigarette companies tried to do the same with smoking, and assume that any use of influence is negative. The fact is, many people in all levels of our society have misused the power of perception, and our culture suffers the consequences. The pornography industry uses perception to legitimize what they do; casinos never mention the high level of gambling-related suicides; and even street-level cocaine dealers use perception to make drug use seem attractive.

I've had the opportunity to teach these principles around the world, and one of my favorite places to lecture is Russia, where I've taught media and broadcasting techniques in Moscow and St. Petersburg. When you study the history of Communism in the former Soviet Union, you'll find that Lenin was a master of perception, and he used these techniques in a negative way to keep millions of people under the brutal hand of the Soviet state. Lenin always felt that cinema was the greatest art form, because he understood the power of movies to inspire, motivate and educate. Under his control, the Russian film industry grew at an enormous rate but was used as a terrible tool to help subjugate the Russian people for decades.

In our home, we've mounted a large Soviet-era political poster promoting the use of cinema, which I found in a Moscow antiques market. The poster features an actress in a highly dramatic pose. The quote in the Russian language is from Lenin himself: "Of all the arts, cinema is the greatest."

In spite of its abuse, the power of perception can be utilized for good if we know how to activate it in our lives. The way to do that is to consider your audience before crafting your message.

Start Thinking in Reverse

It's not the message you send, it's the message that's received that counts. It doesn't matter how brilliant your sermons are; if your intention is misunderstood by the listener, then you've failed to communicate. That's why I always prefer to start at the receiving end first to make sure my message has the best chance of being received properly. How do I do it? I first consider my audience. I know that every listener is evaluating my message through his or her own framework of life experiences and cultural background, which dictate to a great extent the impact the message will have on him or her.

Years ago, I filmed an American evangelist who was conducting massive crusade meetings in Africa. I noticed that the evangelist was telling uniquely American jokes in his message, the content of which a poor, rural African would know nothing about, but the jokes always got a big laugh. After one of the meetings, I asked the translator if the people really understood the jokes.

He laughed and said, "Absolutely not. When the evangelist sets up the joke, I act like I'm translating, but I'm really telling the people that the evangelist is getting ready to tell a joke. I tell them they won't understand it, but to make him feel welcome in our country, please laugh really hard when I give you the cue for the punch line."

To this day, this particular evangelist thinks he's the funniest guy in Africa.

When it comes to delivering your message—even jokes—know who you're dealing with, and know them as intimately as possible. Whatever your business, make sure you tailor your product, presentation or message to your particular audience. Your approach for selling ice should be dramatically different depending on whether you're selling to nomads in the desert or Inuits at the North Pole.

I always tailor my lectures to a specific audience. Sometimes I speak to corporations; other times I speak to nonprofit or religious groups; and still other times to college students. In each situation, I may deliver the same information, but I consider the audience first and customize the message to reach that audience most effectively. Even on those rare occasions when I'm thrust in front of an audience that I'm not familiar with, I take a moment to ask some important questions:

"How many here are active professionals right now?"

"Who are department managers?"

"How many are pastors or ministry leaders?"

"How many want to become professionals in the field sometime in the future?"

"How many are college students?"

These types of questions allow me to better understand the audience, which in turn helps me focus my content more effectively.

So don't begin with your message; begin with your audience. Think how they could perceive your comments and all the myriad ways they might relate to its content. Then, start preparing your message.

The Importance of Packaging

When I was a kid, television meant three channels. Whoopee. But today, my children have *virtually unlimited channels*. The difference is extraordinary and very important to the way you present your message.

My producing experience in an unlimited-channel universe indicates that people take less than five seconds to decide to watch your "program." That's it. Think about how quickly you handle a TV remote and how little chance you give each program to grab your attention. Audiences today are sophisticated and aren't willing to put up with boring production or low-quality pictures. Therefore, I always advise my media clients that *how a program is packaged is just as important as its content.* For instance, no matter how brilliant the program content might be, it has to be packaged in a high-quality, contemporary and compelling way. Otherwise, the viewer won't watch long enough to hear the content, and that means you've lost your audience.

> *Clothes make the man. Naked people have little or no influence on society.*
>
> **MARK TWAIN**

Packaging simply means the "package" (or presentation) that a program is wrapped around. For example, is the lighting interesting? How about the music? Are the graphics contemporary? What about the editing style? Is it directed and acted well? All these are elements that create a powerful package.

In the same way, you, your church or ministry, and your media outreach need an exciting package in order to be perceived as powerfully as possible. From your website, print materials, radio or TV, what elements combine to make your package great?

Here are a few elements of the package to consider:

How You Look

My father used to say that if you dress like a pauper, you'll never get an audience with the king. Although styles today are much more relaxed than in the past, there are still strong feelings among people about clothes and the impact they have on perception. Even in Hollywood, where jeans are considered "business attire," if you look closely, you'll find those jeans are often surrounded by an exotic leather belt, an expensive linen sport coat, a designer T-shirt, a pair of alligator loafers and a $20,000 watch.

I've always been fascinated with how quickly store clerks jump to my attention when I'm wearing a suit, and how slowly they react when I'm in jeans or casual clothes. No matter how laid back the culture gets, clothes still matter, because it's the first indicator people can see and evaluate. Don't become a clothing snob and use clothes to elevate yourself above others. No one respects a person in the office who uses clothes as a label to separate himself or herself from everyone else. But do know and learn the power of how to dress appropriately, and how clothes can be used to give you access to people, places and events.

Well-dressed British dandy Beau Brummell said, "If people turn to look at you on the street, you are not well dressed." He believed in the power of subtlety, and I wish more pastors and hosts of faith-based television programs today listened to his advice.

> *Make sure you have finished speaking before your audience has finished listening.*
>
> **DOROTHY SARNOFF, OPERA SINGER**

How You Speak

At the highest levels of corporate America, you rarely hear the sound of regional accents. A Southern accent sprinkled with colloquialisms may sound cute in your hometown but may only sound redneck in other venues. Talking like a cast member of *The Sopranos* may be desirable in parts of New Jersey, but in parts of Texas you could be shot on sight.

This is not the place to argue the pros and cons of regional accents. I understand that legendary actor and director Orson Welles thought that a Southern accent was the most beautiful sound on the planet; and being a native of North Carolina, I tend to agree. However, it's important to know when a local accent is perceived as attractive and when it's perceived as ignorant or strange, and how to speak appropriately.

Proper grammar is another important element of speaking that few people take the time to learn. If you want to increase your value and how you are perceived in the eyes of other people, never open your mouth unless you're speaking proper English and using grammatically correct sentences. Remember that in most ministry situations, your speaking voice and your writing abilities are your most important communication tools. Poor grammar muddles your message.

If you need coaching in these areas, take the time to enroll in a local college English class, or sign up with a professional vocal coach or image consultant. No matter how old you are, it's never too late to improve your communication abilities.

I'm always shocked at the number of pastors who don't realize that their speaking voice is their single most important physical tool of ministry. You may be a great prayer warrior, a compelling leader, a strong manager or a deep Bible scholar, and certainly God uses all those skills. But if you can't express those gifts through your speaking, then the impact of your message will be greatly impaired. Your single greatest contact point with most people is in the pulpit. Certainly you minister one on one, you counsel, and you have many personal relationships. But your greatest moment is the moment when you step into the pulpit, because that's when you address the most people with the most powerful and compelling message of all.

In the same way, many would say that the ability to speak publicly is a critical skill for a business executive. Managing a board meeting, leading a team, addressing the employees or speaking to the public are all important leadership skills focused on the ability to communicate effectively.

A pro quarterback wouldn't neglect his passing skills, because that's usually the key to his success. In the same way, your calling, commitment and expertise will never be known or fully understood if you can't express those ideas with clear and understandable pronunciation and accurate grammar.

> *Those that are good manners at the court are as ridiculous in the country, as the behavior of the country is most mockable at the court.*
>
> **WILLIAM SHAKESPEARE**

Appropriate Behavior

Knowing how to act in a variety of situations is a critical element in how you are perceived. Some football coaches are brilliant on the field, but at a dinner party they significantly lack social skills. In the same way, I've met doctors who are known internationally for their medical skills in the operating room, but they are embarrassed and awkward in other situations. In a similar vein, I've known national ministry leaders who were far more comfortable in the pulpit than in any other situation. In fact, some of our best preachers are speechless when away from the pulpit.

If you learn to become comfortable in a wide variety of circumstances, your chances of success will be greatly improved.

At a board meeting, at a formal dinner party, at a fund-raising event or local football game, in a casual social situation or on a business trip, does your behavior reflect the level of success you're working toward?

I read recently of an athletic coach who had just signed a multimillion-dollar contract to move to a major university. Because of his winning record, he had been plucked out of small-college obscurity and landed the job of a lifetime.

On one of his first road trips, he traveled to a sports convention and allowed his behavior to get shockingly out of hand. One night, he started drinking heavily at the hotel bar, then took his assistants to a strip club and ended the fateful evening bringing a handful of strippers back to his hotel room to party for the rest of the night. When the university found out about the incident, he was immediately and publicly fired, his marriage was jeopardized if not destroyed and the pending multimillion-dollar contract was ripped to shreds. His life of coaching promise was ruined because of an inability to control his behavior away from the office.

If you travel much for business, you no doubt have heard of the mythical "Hundred Mile Rule," which supposedly states that when a traveling businessperson is beyond a hundred miles from home, what happens on the road stays on the road, and all moral and ethical restraints can be tossed out the window. Whoever came up with that idea was an idiot. Ethical and moral standards have no boundary. The coach in my earlier story was an example of just how much impact your behavior on the road has on your personal and business life.

The "Hundred Mile Rule" has no doubt destroyed thousands of marriages, ruined careers and crippled promising futures. If you're playing fast and loose with your marriage, your relationships or your ethics, I encourage you to reconsider your behavior, and do it right now. Please do not think the value of "perception" is the ability to hide the fact that in reality you are unethical or dishonest. Ethical and moral behavior matters. It creates trust, loyalty and integrity, and when damaged, reputations are difficult if not impossible to rebuild.

Who you are is important; but you can never underestimate the value of how you are perceived.

CHAPTER FOUR

A NEW RELIGION

Brands are belief systems.
PATRICK HANLON

In some cases this is so powerful that the brand becomes more than a brand, and it becomes a way of life.
MARTIN LINDSTROM

There's a new school of thought within the branding and marketing community that has connected successful branding with religious belief. The sense of belonging, the feeling of community, the collective rituals, the shared belief system all point to branding becoming a type of religious experience in America. While that concept might be difficult to swallow for a person of serious religious faith, it does present some intriguing parallels that are difficult to ignore. In many ways, corporate America is subtly attempting to replace religion with branding, at least in the West. In past eras, we might think of ourselves in terms of our religious community; but today Methodist, Baptist, Assembly of God or Lutheran affiliations have given way to Ralph Lauren, Diesel or Lexus.

Just yesterday I overheard a conversation between two businessmen about watches. After comparing their very expensive timepieces, one of the men said, "Well, I've just always thought of myself as a Rolex man." To which the other replied, "I think I'm more of a Breitling man myself." Whatever criteria they used to define a "Rolex man" or a "Breitling man," you can be sure it was based on very strategic advertising strategy, from two companies that understand the power of branding.

Today, brands are the tool for defining our place in the culture, and they have given our capitalist society markers for determining who we are, where we belong and our status in relation to others.

Branding helps us express ourselves to the greater community of believers. Knowing that a friend is a Levi's person or a Nike person helps us understand who they are and what values they represent. Target is the store that sells "mass with class" because it represents high fashion on a limited budget. In a similar way, IKEA has touched a nerve with young couples looking for hip contemporary furniture without the hefty price tag.

In fact, truly successful brands give the impression that there is simply no substitute for what they offer, whether it's a service, product or company. A particular brand becomes a "must-have" in the minds of the public.

Brand communicates ideas, values and standards. What a generation ago was expressed through religious affiliation is now communicated through what we wear, the car we drive and the pen that sits in our pocket.

To a secular culture, brands and religion have merged. The truth is, savvy marketers and advertisers have tapped into our global human aspirations for a sense of belonging, value, meaning and worship, and have turned ordinary, everyday products into brands—and eventually, brands into religions.

In a secular society, brands are worshiped as gods. We value them, express loyalty to them and associate with others of like-minded belief. In major American cities, people have been killed for designer handbags, athletic shoes or jeans. The right brands are sometimes coveted more than human life; and at the altar of validation, blood can be spilled as a sacrifice to the trendy.

The Age of the Brandasaurus

Here's where branding studies get tricky. There's no question that there is a dark side to the world of the brand, and critics of branding are many. Brands have distorted the buying and selling of goods and services, hyping products based not on intrinsic usefulness or value, but on desire alone. Branding has perpetuated the buying and selling of our young people through commercial manipulation and distortion. It has created global corporations whose products are manufactured in Asian sweatshops by underage children making pennies a day. And it has distorted our priorities, making us believe that without this or that product, our lives will be meaningless and empty.

It's hard to argue with critics like Naomi Klein, author of *No Logo*, who calls our culture "The Age of the Brandasaurus."

But there are two different things working here: (1) the power of creating a compelling story around a product, organization or person, and (2) the unethical business practices of corporations around the world. As companies build their organizations into global behemoths, they often trade their integrity for the ability to mass market products. As a person of faith, there is no middle ground in our battle to help everyone reach a standard of living that allows him or her to move out of poverty. Any breach of that standard—whether it be exploiting workers, taking advantage of employees or breaking the law—is out of the question. The more we create decent working and living environments for people, the more we become the people God intends us to be.

I believe that we can understand and use the principles of branding without resorting to corporate dishonesty. As branding expert Wally Olins suggests:

> The weakness of the Naomi Klein school of anti-capitalists is to treat brands as though their only manifestation is corporate and commercial. The influence, strategies and tactics of branding now go way beyond this. Branding is playing a large and increasing part in politics, the nation, sports, culture, and the volunteer sector.[1]

And I would add the "religious" world as well. Telling the story about a product and how it interacts and connects with a consumer doesn't have to be a debasing or dehumanizing experience. The key is in understanding how the media works and using it with integrity and authenticity.

Branding as Meaning

In *Consuming Faith: Integrating Who We Are with What We Buy,* Tom Beaudoin wrote:

> I try to show that one reason the brand economy "works" is that it brings a similar sort of meaningful order and coherence to people's lives that classic spiritual disciplines did in the past (and still do for some today). This is not to make apologies for the brand economy, but to show that it is a spiritual force to be reckoned with, and that people are not idiotic dupes of advertisers but soulfully hungry persons looking for a way to bring a sense of meaningful discipline to their lives. Maybe the

> brand economy and traditional spiritual disciplines have some things to learn from each other.[2]

Bringing meaning to life is one of the reasons I'm so passionate about branding and helping others understand how we can use these principles to reach today's culture. Frankly, the Church has done a poor job of communicating with the culture, and it often comes from not understanding what questions fill the public's mind.

Simply put, I think too many religious leaders are answering questions the culture isn't asking.

For instance, from a media perspective, I've been somewhat dismayed and frustrated at the Church's in-house battle over postmodernism. Yes, we're certainly in that era, but rather than uniting to impact a postmodern culture, we're spending most of our time in-fighting about what postmodernism is, who's too postmodern, and who's not postmodern enough.

There's no question that religious doctrine is important. What we believe about God impacts the way we share Him with others. Our evangelism is handicapped if we don't believe the right things about who God is and what exactly being a Christian means. Today, far too many pastors don't take education seriously, so we have popular pastors preaching serious doctrinal errors—and some actually make fun of seminary training.

As a result, too many people today claim to be Christians but are indistinguishable from nonbelievers. Studies show that many Christians—even pastors—regularly view pornography; and Christians now tend to get divorced as much as non-Christians. It's become so bad that evangelical researcher George Barna says that "close to 9 out of 10 born again Christians in the U.S. have values, lifestyles and attitudes that are indistinguishable from those of non-born again Americans."[3]

Deeds Versus Creeds

On the other hand, real action in the cause of Christ is important as well. What you believe becomes irrelevant if you don't act on your Christian convictions. Pastor Rick Warren says that we've moved from a religion of *creeds* to a religion of *deeds*. One thing the postmodern mind responds to is seeing believers live out their faith.

The massive influx of churches offering assistance to the victims of Hurricane Katrina made a far more positive impact on the culture than years of preaching against abortion, homosexual marriage or euthanasia. Glenn Reynolds, law professor and blogger for Instapundit.com, wrote, "When you look at who was providing relief after Katrina, there's not much in the way of secular humanism to be found."

The key is balance between what we believe and what we do—teaching right doctrine and living out our faith in the public square.

I'm all for the postmodern debate. With a Ph.D. in theology, I can't get enough of a good doctrinal discussion. But I'm also concerned that while we fixate on post*modernism*, we miss something far more important: We've shifted to a post-*Christian* society.

Most people don't understand our evangelical language (what does "born again" mean?), don't care about our priorities (the Ten Commandments in schools?), and certainly don't follow our rules (the Bible). As a result, I see pastors engage the culture using Scripture to support their arguments even though their opponents don't recognize the Bible as authoritative. They use religious language even though the audience has no clue what the words mean. And we've lost touch with how we're perceived by the culture—all of which causes the culture to simply dismiss us as out of touch, or worse, nuts.

When I was growing up, the vast majority of people in our community respected the church; even if they didn't attend church, they honored Christian values and generally had a biblical worldview.

That's not the case anymore. While we're busy having an in-house argument about postmodernism, the culture has already passed us by. To keep the conversation with the culture going, we need to remember that the postmodern debate is an in-house issue. It's an important discussion among believers, but we can't let it distract us from our mission.

As Paul did in Acts 17, to engage a post-Christian culture we need to speak in a language they understand, respect their values (even if we don't agree with them) and be compelling enough to justify their attention.

Just as important, no one in my experience was ever won to Christ through humiliation or embarrassment. So the next time you have a chance to ridicule a nonbeliever, think twice about its effectiveness.

As much as I'd love to go back to a world that respects and values Christian principles, the truth is, we live in occupied territory. If we're going to be successful in communicating a message of hope, we need to realize that the culture doesn't think the way we do. To make an impact, we must take the time and effort to understand, relate to and love the very people who may think we're crazy.

Telling that story effectively is the heart of branding.

The Tenets of "Brand Faith"

The more I study branding as it relates to nonprofits, churches and ministries, the more I'm drawn back to religion itself. Over and over, secular branding experts point to religious faith as the template for real branding. In his book *Primal Branding*,

Patrick Hanlon, founder and CEO of Thinktopia, Inc., has discovered a remarkable parallel between branding and religious faith. In what Hanlon calls "The Primal Code," he finds seven points where successful branding and religion intersect.[4]

1. The Creation Story

Just like the great faiths of the world, every successful product needs a creation story. Whether it's the legendary story of Ray Kroc walking into a McDonald's Brothers restaurant and marveling at the food delivery system they created; a track coach using a waffle iron to create a revolutionary rubber sole for track shoes; or the secret recipe for Coke, a product's "creation story" holds a great mystery, fascination and attraction for most people.

It happens all the time in the Christian ministry world: Joyce Meyer conducting small meetings in motel banquet rooms with a beat-up rental trailer of books and tapes; newspaper magnate William Randolph Hearst's command to "puff Graham" at the beginning of Billy Graham's ministry; Oral Roberts's healing from childhood tuberculosis; Joel Osteen's father, John, starting what would become the largest church in America in an abandoned feed store on Mother's Day, 1959. These are all stories that capture the hearts and imagination of church members, ministry supporters and the public at large.

The creation story can be renewed as well from generation to generation. When Texas pastor John Osteen was nearing the end of his life, he begged his youngest son, Joel, to preach for him. Joel, having spent most of his life as his father's television producer, had no desire to preach, and gently rebuffed his father time after time. Finally, as his dad was nearing death, Joel relented and agreed to preach one Sunday morning. After setting up a phone line so that his father could listen to the service live from the hospital, Joel preached his first sermon. What he didn't realize at the time was that it would also be the last sermon his father ever heard.

Joel went on to build Lakewood Church into the largest place of worship in the United States, and the story of his first sermon has become one of the fascinating anecdotes that surround the ministry.

What's your creation story? Have you kept it alive and in front of people?

Early in my career, I worked with evangelist Oral Roberts at the peak of his ministry when he was producing prime-time TV specials on national television. At the time, I grew weary of his constantly retelling the story of his healing from childhood tuberculosis and his calling into ministry. In the studio, I would tell him over and over, "Oral, give it a rest." But now, looking back, I understand his desire to keep the story in the forefront of his supporters' minds to let them know they were a part of a great ministry that was birthed inside a miracle.

As Patrick Hanlon teaches, creation stories tell the "who" and the "why" and give the consumer a basis for trust in the product. In your ministry, your creation story tells about God's calling, the foundation of your church or ministry and the platform for your convictions.

2. The Creed

Just as the great religions have statements of faith, or sets of doctrinal beliefs, so too do great brands. "It's the real thing." "Save the Whales." "Just Do It." "Think Different." In each case, the words are more than a tagline; they become the rallying cry of the brand. A great tagline calls people to action, gives them a purpose, and defines who they are. In the world of secular products, it might be a tagline that's used with advertising, or a private creed that motivates employees. Sometimes it is both.

Take the line for Absolut Vodka: "How big can we get before we get bad?" This question is not something you necessarily want the public to know, but it's a great motivating creed inside the company. Creeds call people to action, motivate employees and customers, and define who you are and why you exist.

3. The Icons

In Hanlon's world, icons are most often the logos of an organization or product. I'll talk about logos in detail later, but for now, a mark or logo is a simple visual expression of your brand. It's easy to recognize (think about the Nike swoosh), and it's simple to understand. Sometimes icons evolve from print and become larger, like the start-up "bong" on an Apple Computer, or the Budweiser Clydesdale horses. Essentially, an icon is the simplest way to express your brand, your values and your essence to the customer.

Logos are highly misunderstood in the church and ministry world. To use a logo effectively, it has to be greater than a cute symbol. It must express in that simple package the essence of who you are and how you can change someone's life—a big challenge to be sure, but that's the goal.

What's the point? After a month filming in Nigeria during a military coup; and after having a cameraman arrested, spending thousands in bribes to get him out; and after being hungry, dirty and exhausted, I can't express the emotions I felt when I walked out on the airport concourse in Lagos and saw the AA logo on the tail of the American Airlines plane that was going to take me home.

How desperately have you looked for a Starbucks logo when traveling? The key to a logo is immediate recognition. If your logo is so cool and hip that no one knows what it is, you've failed. And if people love the design but don't understand the meaning of the logo, you've failed again.

4. The Rituals

Life is full of rituals—weddings, graduations, religious services, and more. But when it comes to consumer products, Hanlon believes that repeated interaction with a product or company creates an important ritual as well. In *Primal Branding*, Hanlon describes how companies like Unilever and General Motors have actually hired anthropologists to study the rituals involved with their products, whether it's the laundry process or driving a Chevy.

After the terrorist attacks of 9/11, the process of airline travel has become a massive ritual involving purchasing a ticket, learning what we can and can't take on the plane, what to check, dealing with security screenings, waiting for the departure. Today airlines spend enormous amounts of time understanding the ritual and trying to make it as pleasant and quick as possible under the circumstances.

Rituals have been part of the fabric of religious experience since God told Adam and Eve how to live in the Garden. Since that time, the Church has developed elaborate rituals regarding worship, music and various forms of liturgy that have helped believers navigate the faith. Rituals give form to ideals and allow physical actions to convey meaning.

Although "high church" rituals are what most people think of when it comes to Christianity, the truth is, even the most contemporary service has repeated routines that help the congregation. From greeting the visitors, finding nursery facilities and joining the choir, to the educational programs of the church, helping your members understand and grow comfortable with these actions are a critical key to their involvement. It's not a matter of hiring an "efficiency expert" to make confusing routines simple and easy. The challenge is how to inject meaning into the rituals, making them part of the overall worship experience.

From a media ministry perspective, it's no different. How the consumer contacts your ministry, the way they navigate your website, order books and materials, attend conferences, or the many other encounters they may have with the organization, are all things to consider. It's not a matter of being slick; it's a matter of making it worth the trouble. Giving meaning to routine actions is what makes the difference.

5. The Pagans, or Nonbelievers

Hanlon's branding ideas also intersect with religious faith when it comes to nonbelievers. In the marketing world, he's talking about people who don't use the product: the "heathens" and "idolaters," as he calls them. (Heard those terms before?)

To define who you are, you must define who you aren't.

In the marketplace it's about Republicans and Democrats, pro-life and pro-choice, hawks and doves, health-food nuts and fast-food lovers, digital marketing and traditional retailing, New York and Los Angeles, drinkers and nondrinkers, smokers and nonsmokers, and on and on.

As Hanlon says, "We live in a world that has defined itself by contrast and paradox for thousands of years."[5] Traditionally, Christians have not been hesitant to point out sin in the culture, but lately, we see that happening less and less. To a great extent, that happened because society has turned away from preachers who hammer on them with messages about hell and damnation. As the culture locks itself into a "What's in it for me?" mentality, they obviously want to hear less and less about what they're doing wrong or what judgment might be waiting for them after this life.

I've traditionally been one to focus on the positive. I worry that if Christians continue to focus on the negative, we'll become known as "the people who are against everything." When that happens, it becomes easier and easier for the culture to turn us off.

We offer the greatest gift of all time, so I want to define the Body of Christ as people who are *for* something, not *against* everything. But if Hanlon is correct, being clear about what we're against isn't always a bad thing.

I think the lesson here is that defining the nonbelievers isn't really about condemning them; it's about identifying them. Once we can define who the nonbelievers are, we can better focus on the options for reaching that particular audience. That's why doctrinal ignorance can be so damaging. In order to express our message properly, we need to believe the right things. In a world where far too many pastors discount a strong theological education, we're developing a generation of pastors who are ignorant of the basic principles of the faith. As a result, we don't know who we are, and we certainly can't identify who we aren't.

One of the big alarms that Philip Kenneson and James Street sound in their book *Selling Out the Church: The Dangers of Church Marketing* is pursuing demographic groups. They feel that trying to measure target audiences is futile, largely because who are we to decide who the Holy Spirit convicts and doesn't convict? Plus, does measuring lead to marginalizing? By targeting specific demographic groups, are we marginalizing others?

These are important questions and concerns, but one thing I've learned in more than 30 years of working with churches and ministries is that each one has its own unique personality. Based on many things, such as the style of worship, the personality of the pastor, the geographic location and the denomination, each church seems to reflect the make-up of its particular congregation.

Because of those unique differences, I think it's completely appropriate for the evangelistic outreach of the church to focus first on those who might be more compatible with that church's personality. Certainly we want to welcome anyone to the service and reach out to a broad range of the public. But just as a secular business goes after the low-hanging fruit, it's perfectly appropriate for a hip, contemporary church to start with reaching out to singles; or an inner-city church to evangelize in the inner city.

That begins by knowing who you are and who you aren't. Again, defining in this way is not meant to *exclude* but to better *include*. Knowing who you aren't helps you define who you are.

6. The Sacred Words

Every great product experience comes with its own language or lingo. Where would Starbucks be without a Grande No-Foam Latte, a Tall Wet Skinny Cap, or a Mocha? McDonald's has a Big Mac; Apple has an entire vocabulary of terms; and just try to read the shorthand your teenager uses to send a text message on his or her cell phone.

Christianity has the ultimate sacred vocabulary in the Bible, and its impact on Western culture has been unprecedented. From the moment when William Tyndale began translating the Bible into English, he began to transform the language and change the world. Chuck Stetson, founder of The Bible Literacy Project in New York City has stated that Western literature, education, art, music and more would be dramatically different without the language of the Bible. There are thousands of biblical references in Shakespeare alone, and you can find biblical allusions in the greatest novels throughout history.

However, the language of Christianity is losing its currency in the world. As a result, Stetson created a foundation that published *The Bible and Its Influence*, a secondary school textbook to help public schools understand the heritage of the Bible. Without attempting to proselytize or convert, the book simply takes a student through Western history, showing them the myriad examples of how Judeo-Christian ideals and values have shaped the West, and the influence of the Bible through the centuries. It's a staggering project with incredible implications.

After William Tyndale translated the Bible into English, for the first time the English-speaking people had a common story. The Bible became the most widely read book in history, because it was the thread that held together the English-speaking peoples. Its publication sparked an explosion of literacy, because generations of children were taught how to read by using Bible passages and memorizing Scripture. Its influence cannot be argued. But today, that influence is waning.

When my daughters were in high school, they were amazed at the number of students who had no idea what Christmas or Easter really meant, or had no concept of the Nativity or the Resurrection. They might have been *A* students in school, but they were illiterate when it came to the Bible.

A few years ago, I saw this challenge firsthand when I went shopping in the jewelry district in downtown Los Angeles. If you want a great price on jewelry, this is the place to come. It's a multi-block area of L.A. that's filled with watch and jewelry dealers, and it's an experience all its own.

I drove down secretly one morning to look for a Christmas gift for my wife, Kathleen. As I was shopping, I began watching a young couple looking for a necklace. The dealer brought out a beautiful tray of cross necklaces ranging from simple contemporary designs to more traditional designs featuring Jesus hanging on the cross. The young couple was very impressed, and as they looked down the row of crosses, the woman became interested in the Catholic-looking style design with the figure of Jesus on the cross.

She looked puzzled and said to the salesman, "I don't understand. Who's that little guy hanging on that cross necklace?"

She was at least 25 years old but had absolutely no idea who that "little guy" was or what He was doing on that necklace.

That's the culture we are trying to reach. The sacred words we use have little meaning anymore. To reach this generation, we first need to reenergize the meaning of sacred language in order to give the words value to people like that woman in the jewelry store.

7. The Leader

The last comparison point for Hanlon is the leader. In the secular world, you have to go no further than Walt Disney, Bill Gates, Steve Jobs, Jack Welch, Oprah, or Thomas Edison. When it comes to values, names like Dr. Martin Luther King Jr., George Washington, Mother Teresa or Billy Graham appear. These are leaders that define organizations, products or ideals.

A great leader is often what causes a company to transcend the marketplace and create an emotional connection in the mind of the consumer. A recent article in *Fast Company* magazine stated, "Research suggests that brands that engage consumers emotionally can command prices as much as 20% to 200% higher than competitor's and sell in far higher volumes."[6]

Occasionally, I've been asked to be the master of ceremonies at different organization's events. Although I enjoyed it, in certain situations, I felt that it was unfortunate the organization didn't have their own dynamic and charismatic leader to do the job instead of an outsider. For the organization's leader to be at the podium, having the audience identify him or her with the vision, would have been so much greater than simply using a fill-in like me for the job.

Vision is what great leadership is all about; and while businesses are filled with experienced managers, most lack a strong vision to take them to the next level. As the Bible says, "Without a vision the people perish."

In the Christian world, ultimate leadership and vision is found in Jesus Christ; but on the earth, we've entrusted that vision to pastors and ministry leadership. When the structure of the Early Church was set up in the New Testament, there was a need for men and women of vision, integrity and compassion. That need is still the same today.

The same holds true for nonprofit organizations. The strongest humanitarian organizations are ones that are led by visionary men and women who know how to make a connection with their donors.

Whenever possible, I make an organization's leader an integral part of the brand because people want to identify with a person, not a building, program, or radio or television program. I cannot stress enough that today's churches and nonprofits need strong leaders. Call them "servant leaders" if you like, but leaders nonetheless. Within a great brand is often a great leader who is able to personally identify with the purpose and reason the organization exists, and that makes a powerful connection with the audience.

> *My father always said not to talk about religion, politics and money. So right here and now I'm going to break the first rule by revealing some of my most fascinating revelations by placing branding in, dare I say, a religious context.*
>
> **MARTIN LINDSTROM, BRANDING CONSULTANT**

Branding Revelations

While Patrick Hanlon has written the definitive book on connecting the dots between successful branding and religious belief, he's certainly not the only one crying in the wilderness. Brand futurist Martin Lindstrom has written extensively on the religious context of branding at his website at *martinlind strom.com*.

Lindstrom writes that he discovered the connection between religion and branding when watching young girls on the streets of Tokyo dressed head to toe in Hello Kitty items. Apparently, nothing they carried or wore was left unbranded, even down to the Hello Kitty nails, Hello Kitty earrings, and Hello Kitty cell phones. Having had two daughters who went through the Hello Kitty craze, I could relate.

This and similar observations left him wondering, "What makes people go that far? What are the ingredients that make up such an extreme brand obsession? And ultimately, what can the world of advertising learn from this when setting out to build a brand?"

After embarking on a journey to discover the ingredients that created strong religious faith, Lindstrom discovered 10 remarkable parallels between faith and branding. I like the fact that he takes great pains to indicate he doesn't believe that religious faith has actually learned anything from branding, but there's no question in his mind that branding has definitely been inspired by faith. While a few of Lindstrom's parallels are similar to Hanlon's primal branding list, I thought they were unique enough for this discussion. These could be called Martin Lindstrom's "10 Commandments of Branding."

1. A Sense of Belonging

Martin Lindstrom likes to use Weight Watchers as an example. With more than two million members, it's all about receiving advice and support from others in the program. The encouragement and inspiration of peers can make a significant difference in motivation. In truth, outside of family, the Church may be the original and most effective community of all. Throughout history, the Church has been involved in helping families through the most difficult aspects of life.

I was watching a movie recently that illustrated just how much the church community helps during a crisis. After a funeral service, one of the characters said, "That's what we do—after the funeral, we come over and sit. We also bring a casserole." It was comedic line, but it made me remember all the times growing up that church members would "go and sit" with people going through a crisis. A sense of belonging is critically important in a religious community, and to brands as well.

2. A Clear Vision

Lindstrom often refers to Steve Jobs's potent vision for Apple Computer that began in the 1980s. A clear and powerful vision is a key part of any successful company—particularly companies that become legends. A strong vision is timeless and transcends trends, fashion and culture change. From a religious perspective, it's not just about romantic stories such as Joan of Arc. Some of our greatest hospitals, universities and other social institutions began from a religious vision to impact the lives of people.

3. Power from the Enemy

Competition fuels global business. Coke versus Pepsi. Coors versus Budweiser. Apple versus Microsoft. Home Depot versus Lowes. The list is endless. In fundraising for nonprofit or religious causes, we know that creating an enemy increases response—whether that enemy is another political party, an ideological position or a vice. The ongoing battle of sin versus salvation is the keystone of the Christian faith, and business leaders can learn much from understanding the "other."

4. Authenticity

Lindstrom is particularly eloquent here: "Authenticity is hard to define. Is Las Vegas or canned laughter authentic? Without thinking, you may initially answer no; but a reconsidered answer might just be yes. Are the Olympics authentic? This answer to this is unambiguously yes, because the Olympics contain the four defining components of authenticity. It's *real*, it's *relevant*, it has *rituals* and it's part of a story. More and more brands are required to be authentic—just like religion." People have always responded to faith when it seems real and relevant to their lives.

5. Consistency

In a world of constant, technological change, it's nice to feel the comfort of consistency. Throughout the ages, the religious community has been a consistent and reassuring force in the lives of people, and business brands are just beginning to notice. Whether it's the ease of ordering your coffee the exact same way at any Starbucks in the world, finding the same Big Mac or navigating your new software, people are looking for the least difficult and most familiar path. Brand consistency extends throughout the customer experience, from store design, product operation, ordering, design issues, and more. Be innovative and creative, but don't forget to be consistent.

6. Perfection

Lindstrom notes that there are as many as 521 websites dedicated solely to how to polish the engine of a Harley Davidson. For a real fan, this attention to detail isn't an option. I have a friend who's a fanatic audiophile. The detail he looks for in a new music system is phenomenal—if not infuriating. That's why we're seeing such strong growth in "luxury" brands: high-end watches, handbags, fashion, and even writing pens. People who are fans search for perfection and are willing to go to great lengths—and pay great money—to get it.

7. Symbols

I've produced television and film programming in more than 40 countries around the world. Not long ago, I traveled more than 250,000 air miles in a single year. Business is now global, and that means that what we encounter in the global arena needs to be as simple as possible. From transportation signs, computer software, weights and measures and more, symbols are more important than ever to reach a global audience. Just like illiterate Russians used icons (biblical scenes painted on pieces of wood) to help them understand Bible stories, symbols have been pervasive throughout the history of the Church. The cross, the bread and wine, the altar, the dove are just a few of the many symbols that express different aspects of the Christian faith. Symbols help a product—just like a religious faith—to be understood in the swirl of cultural and technological change.

8. Mystery

The transcendent mystery of faith has been discussed, debated and studied since the beginning of mankind. Mystery matters, and people are endlessly fascinated with the spiritual and mysterious. In business, there are plenty of highly protected mysteries—from McDonald's secret sauce to KFC's secret spices, the Coca-Cola formula and even computer operating systems. Some are real and some are myth, but adding the element of mystery to a product or organization heightens the fun and excitement and creates a desire to explore more deeply.

9. Rituals

The power of ritual is one of the least understood aspects within the world of branding. The Catholic Church has always understood the awesome power of ritual, and I'm seeing a growing trend of Christians moving into churches today with more liturgical traditions. In the business world, I've discovered that I always get better results when I order my coffee in exactly the right sequence: "Iced, grande, soy, latte." On the plane, if I order Club Soda, they always ask if I want a lime or a lemon. The Apple "bong" when a computer program starts is another example. Rituals become expected, and as such, they can become a key part of the fabric of the marketing experience.

10. Sensory Appeal

In liturgical churches, they sometimes refer to this as the "smells and bells." For thousands of years, religious communities have understood the power of engaging a worshiper's sense of smell, sound, sight and taste. It creates the sense you're in another world and lifts you into a more focused worship experience. As Lindstrom noted, the rise in "flagship" stores for companies such as Nike, Disney or Apple Computer help a customer move from the everyday world into a new brand experience. Stores like Victoria's Secret or Bath and Body Works further enhance the experience with smells. The background music is also highly researched in an attempt to sooth and motivate the customer but not distract him or her from the buying experience. It's about intensifying the sensations around the product and creating a unique sensory encounter. So the next time you walk into an Apple Computer store, remember that they're taking their cues from thousands of years of Church history.[7]

Is Branding a Religion?

In Lindstrom's words, "Whether we love it, or hate it, the world of branding is becoming increasingly inspired by the world of religion. Religion offers a powerful roadmap for how branding can evolve over the years to come. All it needs to do is look to the ancient ingredients that make up religious followings. In some cases this is so powerful that the brand becomes more than a brand, and it becomes a way of life."[8]

When I first encountered the writings of Patrick Hanlon and Martin Lindstrom, I realized that Christians should have known this all along. The story of the Christian faith is filled with all the elements that connect with a person, offer conviction and cause a change in his or her heart and life. Ultimately, Christianity is about change. Although "conversion" has become a bad word in this supposedly "tolerant" society, the truth is, "conversion" and "repenting" mean that you change your thinking.

The Holy Spirit has been helping people do that for centuries and, finally, the marketing world has discovered its impact.

CHAPTER FIVE

TELLING YOUR STORY

Every time you use the word "brand," mentally replace it with the word "image" or "reputation."
WALLY OLINS, CHAIRMAN OF SAFFRON BRAND CONSULTANTS

There's something evangelistic about what we do.
LLOYD HILL, CEO, APPLEBEE'S RESTAURANTS

Nike, Starbucks, Apple Computer, IBM. All it takes is a logo, and you know the exact company represented and what the logo means. Not long ago I was driving in St. Louis and saw a white roadside billboard with nothing on it but the Nike swoosh. No letters, no pictures, just the swoosh. At that moment, I realized that the vast majority of people who drive past that billboard know exactly what company is represented and the meaning of the symbol. At the same time, the phrase "Just Do It" probably races through their minds. That's the power of a compelling brand.

What if your church or nonprofit organization had that same kind of visual recognition in your community? What if your story, purpose and meaning were so clear that all it took was a simple graphic design to remind people about you and your message?

Some simple searching on the Internet reveals the Nike brand statement:

The spirit of the athlete.

It doesn't say anything about shoes, quality or price, and yet it expresses the company and its vision perfectly. Everything Nike does is caught up in that simple phrase.

Notice, by the way, that the mission statement isn't the phrase "Just Do It." That's a tagline. A tagline is a public statement that expresses the brand through advertising and promotion. The brand statement is normally for insiders—people inside the company—to help them understand the identity you've created.

Taglines can be used for individual advertising campaigns and can change as advertising and marketing concepts change. These slogans are more flexible and can be very effective.

Some of the earliest advertising slogans can be traced to the late 1890s when business leaders realized the power of emotion to sell products. The website "taglineguru.com" keeps a listing of the "100 Most Influential Taglines Since 1948." It's a fascinating list, and I would encourage you to check it out. Here are the top 10 on the list:

1. Got milk? (1993) California Milk Processor Board
2. Don't leave home without it. (1975) American Express
3. Just do it. (1988) Nike
4. Where's the beef? (1984) Wendy's
5. You're in good hands with Allstate. (1956) Allstate Insurance
6. Think different. (1998) Apple Computer
7. We try harder. (1962) Avis
8. Tastes great, less filling. (1974) Miller Lite
9. Melts in your mouth, not in your hands. (1954) M&M Candies
10. Takes a licking and keeps on ticking. (1956) Timex

A brand statement, on the other hand, is an overall identity for the company. Here is Starbucks' brand statement:

A great coffee experience.

That brand statement means so much more than just a good cup of coffee. It resonates throughout the design of the store, the menu selections, the attitude of the employees, the multiple locations, the consistency of the product, and more. I have no idea if it's true, but not long ago I heard a story that a hotshot MBA came into the company and decided to do some cost cutting. I'm told he did a sheet by sheet, roll by roll, store by store study of toilet paper used at the coffee shops and discovered that by changing from two-ply toilet paper to one-ply, he could save the company hundreds of thousands of dollars.

After a major meeting, it was decided that Starbucks would continue to spend the extra money and supply their restrooms with two-ply paper. It was apparently decided that single-ply toilet paper doesn't make for "A Great Coffee Experience."

I'm sure you would agree.

True, or not? I don't know, but it's a perfect example of how the brand statement should permeate every aspect of the organization, ministry or nonprofit. It's not just about the "product"; it's about all the things that happen when a customer comes in contact with your product or company.

Now let's look at how that thinking can impact your particular brand.

Part One: Understanding Who You Are

Whenever my company brands a nonprofit and ministry client, we take them through an extensive Branding Workshop that helps us determine their brand story. We ask the questions:

What is the ultimate expression of the particular church, ministry, pastor or spiritual leader? As a nonprofit, what's your ultimate expression of mission? What are you here to accomplish? What is the brand story you want to communicate to your congregation, television viewers, web surfers, readers or customers?

In other words, *What do they think of when they think of you?*

In these sessions, we always want to be sensitive and compassionate. Successful ministry in the twenty-first century is a complex enterprise; and in a postmodern culture, a thriving outreach is contingent on a number of issues, not the least of which is the grace of God.

I obviously have no control over the client's personal calling or relationship with God. So we concentrate on the aspects we can control and focus on the issues that tell the story most effectively. Our purpose is to discover the story or identity that makes the client different and sets the organization apart.

I'd like to help you do the same. So, if terms like "marketing" or "branding" are still uncomfortable for you, I would encourage you to read on and give it a little time. But from this point on, I'll assume that we're on the same page, and our goal is to determine how to tell the most effective story about who you are, what your ministry is about and how that ministry can impact people's lives.

The Branding Focus

In the religious world, when I work with a particular pastor or ministry leader, it's usually in the context of a media outreach. Our company, Cooke Pictures (cookepictures.com), produces programming and consults with some of the largest churches and ministries in the country on how to improve their effectiveness in the media. The consultation could be a project with television, radio, a website, print media or other emerging media platforms. Our passion is reaching an audience, and we're usually called in when a media ministry has hit a plateau or is having difficulty reaching the next level.

In many cases, we choose to focus our branding on the pastor or ministry leader, not just the church or ministry itself. If your church is in Dallas, and your market is local, then you can focus your marketing efforts on how your *church* impacts that city. But with a media outreach, your viewers or listeners in Los Angeles or Miami don't care about the church; they're interested in what they see on television or hear on radio. Especially when it comes to preaching and teaching ministries, in most cases we've discovered that people tune in to hear the pastor's teaching; so in branding a national media ministry, we usually focus on the personality that leads that ministry. There's no question that we live in a culture of Christian celebrity.

The Cultural Reality of Celebrity

Today, national ministry leaders have become "stars" to the point that they're forced to fly in private jets because they get mobbed at airports. I saw one very vocal woman grab a well-known pastor by the arm in the produce section of a grocery store and loudly beg for his autograph. It was humiliating for the pastor and his family. While most people criticize these leaders, it's the general public that has created the phenomenon. Much like entertainment celebrities in Hollywood, the Christian community has bought into the concept of celebrity in a big way.

I was in a meeting recently with a major ministry figure who happens to be a bestselling author. He's so successful in selling books that the publisher was pushing him to create a series of novels. This particular ministry leader doesn't read novels, doesn't like novels and has no desire to write a novel.

But his readership is so loyal that they would buy anything with his name on it.

So they decided to look for fictional storylines, hire a ghostwriter (a professional writer who writes books for other people) and then have the ministry leader put his name on the finished novel. I'm sure the sales will go through the roof.

This is the dark side of branding. It's done all the time in the secular world. (Do you *really* think professional athletes and movie stars know how to write?) But when it happens in the religious world, it's a little disconcerting to say the least.

Don't Throw the Baby Out with the Bathwater

I encourage an exploration of both sides of any issue. I passionately believe in branding, but it can be abused. At my online blog at philcooke.com, these conversations happen on a regular basis, and the debate and discussions often get pretty passionate in both directions. But just as we don't stop taking an offering at church because some pastors take financial advantage of people, neither do we dump marketing and branding because some choose to use it for manipulation.

Christian celebrity is a fact of life, and we can't control that. So we need to move beyond it to understand the purpose of branding and marketing. I choose to brand *a pastor or ministry leader* in most cases, particularly when the goal is to create a national media outreach. I tend to brand the pastor or ministry leader even when marketing on the local level. In a perfect world, people would come to your church for a multitude of reasons—children's ministry, youth programs, missions, worship, community. In reality, most people first experience a church because of what they hear in the pulpit.

If your church or ministry is in Atlanta, people in Des Moines, Tulsa or Birmingham will probably never come to your church, so focusing on your music, worship or community will mean very little to them. They're usually looking for your personal ministry, and that's why we focus on you. Examples of compelling personal ministries might be pastors like Greg Laurie, Joel Osteen, Ed Young, Mark Crow, Jack Graham or John MacArthur. All have vibrant local churches, but viewers or listeners *outside* their geographical area are more interested in their personal teaching or preaching ministries.

In the past, music was a significant aspect of national radio and television ministries; today we can hear the finest singers and musicians in the world any time of the day on our own CD or digital music player. So having your local choir or special music doesn't make much impact, unless your worship leader is a nationally known personality.

Recently, I visited a church that was voting on calling a new pastor. The church board was supporting a candidate who was highly organized, a great manager and was excellent with people. He had long experience as an administrator, and from that perspective, he was an excellent choice. The only sticky problem was that he was completely inept in the pulpit. His sermons were dry, he couldn't tell stories well and he was embarrassed and awkward on the platform. It was so bad that even loyal members of the congregation were visibly uncomfortable watching him preach.

The board, being concerned about the whole picture, was more than willing to overlook his lack of skill in the pulpit and focus on his abilities managing the church. In a perfect world, that might work. Certainly there are many things that contribute to the worship experience, and the 30-minute message on Sunday shouldn't overpower all the other wonderful aspects of church life.

But I felt compelled to remind them that if church growth was a concern, they should rethink their direction. After all, our experience indicates that the Sunday morning service is the main entry portal for the vast majority of people who visit. Who wants to bring a friend to hear a pastor who can't preach? The 30-minute message on Sunday morning may seem like a small part of the overall experience, but in most cases, it's the pastor in the pulpit who casts the vision for the church, motivates the congregation and inspires growth.

They didn't take my advice, and since that time, the church has been wonderfully managed, but membership, programs and community outreach have all dramatically declined.

I met another pastor who was a wonderful man, but he was one of the worst preachers I've ever met. He loved God and was great with people but was simply a catastrophe in the pulpit. As a result, he had been the pastor of 18 churches in his 21 years of ministry. He kept getting asked to leave because he simply couldn't preach. I was fascinated to find out how long it would take him to realize that perhaps preaching was not his gift.

This book isn't about bad preaching. My point is that while at the local level there are certainly different points of view and various possibilities for branding, one thing I've discovered is that the pastor or ministry leader is the hub of the brand. Everything else revolves around his or her role.

I may take some flak for that thinking, and to be honest, I personally don't like it either. But that's another example of the changes we need to make to reach an audience in a media-driven world. We first must understand how people initially connect and then develop our branding and identity from there.

Another important reason that the pastor or ministry leader is a critical key to branding is that in the media, people ultimately want a relationship with a person—not a program, a building or a ministry. So in order to develop fund-raising, partnership or resource relationships, focusing on the leader is key.

Personal Branding

We call this technique "personal branding." An excellent book on the subject is *The Brand Called You* by Peter Montoya. In his book, Montoya shares three critical insights for personal branding.[1]

1. Visibility Is Just as Important as Ability

In a media-driven culture, being seen is just as important as being effective. There are hundreds of brilliant, gifted pastors who will never make an impact because people don't know who they are. You see the concept illustrated most clearly in Hollywood, where actors of little ability and skill make millions of dollars from being in the right place at the right time. As a producer and director, I'm amazed at the incredible level of talent among unknown actors I see in casting sessions. There are men and women with incredible gifts who will never be recognized or known.

In ministry, the people you see on television or listen to on radio aren't necessarily the most gifted, anointed or skilled ministry leaders out there. But they have influence because they have visibility.

Does ability matter? No question about it. I believe in education, skill, expertise and personal growth. When the door opens, you'd better be ready to act and have the talent and calling to back it up. But unless that door opens, all the talent in the world will do little outside of entertaining your family.

Getting your face out there isn't necessarily the act of an egotistical maniac. Certainly there are narcissists in the media (and plenty on religious television), but the truth is, getting on the radar of the public is the first step toward understanding the power of a compelling personal brand.

2. You Can't Brand a Lie

Certainly, as people of faith, we should act with integrity; and every expression of your ministry should be true. But when it comes to skill and expertise, I find that a great number of ministry leaders take a shortcut. Through advertising and promotion, pastors often indicate areas of expertise they don't really have, or experience that's never actually happened.

As I write this book, the war in Iraq continues to rage, and the terrorist crisis is front-page news. In the context of that national discussion, I recently attended a church conference on the Middle East conflict. The main speaker was a pastor who was positioned in the advertising of the event as an expert on the subject; so I was eager to hear what he had to say. But when he began his talk, he admitted that he had only recently visited Israel for the first time and was so moved during that first visit that he had begun to teach in his Wednesday night service about the church's Jewish roots.

I was shocked, to say the least. Here's a guy who received top billing at a national Christian conference focused on the biblical answer to the Middle East crisis, and yet, as the keynote speaker, he had only visited Israel a few months before (for the first time) and had just recently started exploring the subject.

I walked out of the conference. The Christian community has brilliant scholars on the subject, experts from a variety of perspectives, Jewish and Messianic leaders, and more. But when it came to the expertise of this event's speakers, they chose to brand the conference based on a major stretch of credibility.

Just check out the advertisements for the latest Christian conferences and look for the number of "Dr." degrees. Everybody in ministry is a Doctor of something these days. And don't get me started on the number of "Bishops," "Prophets," "Prophetesses," "Apostles," and more. Some denominations continue to use some of these designations in official ministry capacities, but many simply make it up to sound good.

When the truth is revealed, false branding dies hard. Montoya cites the case of television evangelist Jimmy Swaggart:

> A perfect example is Jimmy Swaggart, the television minister who waged war on evil until he publicly admitted to an unspecified "sin" that later turned out to be cavorting with prostitutes. Despite his famous, tearful "I have sinned against you" speech and his penitence, Swaggart has never rehabilitated his image because so many of his followers felt extremely and irreversibly betrayed.[2]

I don't use that example to criticize Jimmy Swaggart or comment on his sincerity, or his relationship with God. I use the quote as a powerfully clear example of the damage caused when brands are betrayed.

You might remember the famous Tylenol scare in the fall of 1982, when McNeil Consumer Products, a subsidiary of Johnson & Johnson, was hit with a major crisis after seven people on Chicago's West Side died mysteriously. After a brief investigation, it was determined that each of the people had taken an Extra-Strength Tylenol capsule laced with cyanide. When the news of the incident caused a massive, nationwide panic, Johnson & Johnson was forced to act. Realizing that millions of dollars were at stake, they could have hesitated, fought the accusations and held up the investigation. But they immediately pulled millions of dollars of Tylenol from the shelves in a bold move to restore the public's trust. By acting quickly, they accomplished what has since become a lesson in positive public relations.

Today the Tylenol brand is a trusted name because consumers link it with integrity and public trust. Jimmy Swaggart, on the other hand, has never recovered. Today his television program limps along on various stations, and although many years have passed since the revelations of his fall, he has never recovered his place of ministry in the minds of the nationwide Christian audience.

Keep in mind that perception plays a significant role in the process. In 2006, when pastor Ted Haggard resigned from his church in Colorado Springs under a cloud of alleged sexual misconduct, there were multiple issues at play, including how poorly he and his staff handled the media. I'll never forget watching the news broadcast when they featured an interview with Ted after he stopped his car at the end of the driveway with his wife and kids in the backseat. An impromptu interview in the front yard in earshot of the kids wasn't the most appropriate venue to answer questions about alleged sexual wrongdoing.

Who can possibly know how difficult struggling with this issue for years had been, and how humiliating the experience was for Ted and his family. We all struggle with sin in our lives, and it's important to remind ourselves just how easy it is to fall.

This discussion is not meant to be a personal criticism of Ted. But for the Church as a whole, we need to wake up to living and sharing our witness in a media-driven culture. The way the mass media exposes, uncovers and tells the story is vastly different from anything the Church has experienced in 2,000 years of its history. If we don't understand how the media works, it will forever damage our witness to the world.

And it's not about covering up, deflecting or denying. On the contrary, it's about being truthful and confronting the media in a way that permits the real story to be told without letting denials, information scraps, inaccuracies and falsehoods color the story. The stakes are remarkably high. At the time, it didn't take much to see the anti-religious bloggers and writers descending on the Haggard story like sharks to blood. The hypocrisy, denials and botched releases energized Christianity's critics, and it was hard to blame them.

In fact, it was sobering to note an America Online poll that asked 185,364 people what they thought of Ted's confession. In my opinion, largely because of the poor handling of the story,

65 percent of the respondents said they believed his confession was insincere, and only 35 percent felt it was sincere.[3]

We have to take the media seriously and understand how to effectively communicate today. During the weeks after the story broke, "Ted Haggard" was the most searched name on multiple search engines, and Technorati.com revealed that it was the number one topic among bloggers. That means that in spite of the war in Iraq, and on the eve of a national mid-term election, this was the number one priority for the American people. Millions of people were asking about it, searching for information and writing about the issue. But the Sunday morning after the story broke, I visited a church here in Los Angeles, and the pastor never even mentioned it. Not once. It was the most asked question on people's minds in the country, and this pastor chose not to engage in a conversation about sin, denial, forgiveness, restoration and salvation—or even offer to pray for Ted and his family. What a missed opportunity!

This is why so many in the culture think the church is irrelevant. The world is asking questions, but we refuse to deal with them.

It's also not simply about moral failure; it's about gifts, talents and expertise. If you bill yourself as an expert on drug treatment, you'd better be able to back it up. If you want to become known for family ministry, you'd better have the credentials to prove it. If you teach on financial success, you'd better be rich.

We need to be reminded that there's no substitute for real experience and accomplishment. When we see ministry leaders on television, it's easy to think it must be simple to do what they're doing. But we often forget about the years or, sometimes, decades they spent in the trenches of education and ministry learning the principles that allow them to minister at an influential national level.

In this age of the Internet, anyone can be investigated, any time, with a few easy keystrokes on a computer. Politicians are finding this out in the heat of campaigns, as old DUI convictions suddenly pop up, a racist remark is uncovered or embarrassing academic records are revealed. Shortly after celebrity *Playboy* model Anna Nicole Smith died in the Bahamas, the celebrity gossip site TMZ.com revealed photos from her refrigerator allegedly showing drugs that she was supposedly taking at the time of her death. Likewise, major corporations struggle as confidential internal memos are released on the Internet as quickly as they're distributed to employees.

We live in a world of video cameras, databases and information retrieval. Never in history have religious and nonprofit leaders needed to be more transparent. In fact, Internet search engines aren't about "search"; they're about "reputation management." For a generation of young people who grew up posting the most intimate details of their lives on the Web, they're finding that in their twenties, it's getting tough to find a job. Once the interview is complete, the first thing a future employer often does is Google them, only to find the old drinking photos from the college dorm, a raging political rant, embarrassing personal details, explicit sexual writing, and more.

Hardly welcome news for a prospective employer.

In the old days, executives, pastors and nonprofit leaders could have a private jet, a luxury car or a mansion, and few would ever find out. But today, a few keystrokes on the computer reveal everything.

3. In a Media-driven Culture, Being Different Is Everything

The world isn't looking for a copy of a major religious leader; they're looking for someone new, innovative and original. God gave you unique DNA, so your job is to discover how your unique gifts and talents can differentiate your ministry from everyone else's.

> *Differentiate or die.*
>
> **JACK TROUT, MARKETING CONSULTANT**

You have no idea the number of pastors who call our offices each week asking us to "Do the same thing for us that you did for your national ministry clients." They've got it backward. There's already one of *them*. A new person needs to emphasize his or her unique *differences*.

Besides, each of our clients were unique and brilliant long before I ever met them. Probably the most powerful gift these leaders had was an understanding of who they were and what their talent and calling was about.

In working with these pastors and ministry leaders, I'm reminded of Michelangelo, who was asked about how he carved such brilliant statues of angels. He remarked that he didn't carve statues; he just removed the excess stone so that the angel inside could come out. That's very often the case with our work.

It's not so much a matter of recreating or rebuilding a ministry; it's more about cutting away the junk so that the real ministry that's inside can be released.

And believe me, the junk is there. Lack of professionalism, poor media production, unqualified staff, poor taste, inept leadership, insecurity, small budgets, bad assumptions, and more, plague many organizations today and hamper their effectiveness.

A quick look at Christian television will prove that most ministries are pretty similar in their look, style and presentation.

Few men and women in the ministry world are truly unique and different. God is the great creator, and yet most ministry leaders simply copy what they see on TV or hear on the radio.

Listen to Apple Computer ads and "Think Different." If God created you as a unique individual, what does that mean for the type of vision you're called to accomplish?

The Branding Team

When my company brands a product, person or organization, we usually ask that the people closest to the client (pastor or ministry leader) participate. This almost always includes the spouse and, sometimes, grown or particularly mature children, especially if they work in the ministry. (After all, they've seen the organization from the inside.) Then we ask that key members of the leadership team be present. These staff members are especially important to the process if they know the client closely and have experienced a long working relationship.

Branding Question #1: What's the Point?

When I help a client with branding, I usually begin with a question the secular world of branding doesn't ask (or rarely asks). That question is, *What's the point?* or, *Why are you doing this?* When branding a hammer, a cold medication, a computer or other product, the motivation of the company doesn't mean nearly as much as when branding a church, ministry or nonprofit. With some variation, most consultants in the secular advertising and marketing world refer to a "branding triangle," featuring three questions:

1. *Who are you?*
2. *What are your gifts and talents?*
3. *What makes you unique and different?*

I use these questions, as well, but I prefer to begin with a different question that revolves around the person's calling, motivation and the driving force behind the mission he or she is trying to accomplish. A conversion experience and subsequent ministry calling are certainly important to this question, but the answer usually lies in another area.

For instance, just this morning, I was watching writer and teacher Beth Moore on television. During the program, she talked about her experience as a victim of childhood abuse. She mentioned the encounter as the focal point that drives her ministry today—to the point that not a single day goes by when that incident doesn't come into play somehow in her ministry.

She can understand other victims of abuse because she's been there and understands their pain. Her own experience keeps her from becoming prideful. It helps her minister more effectively because of the way God helped her through the devastating trauma. She went on to say how her past has helped her understand the providence of God, because although God didn't cause the abuse, He's been able to use the experience to make her ministry more effective to millions of women.

She's a bestselling writer, a brilliant speaker and a strong Bible teacher. But her childhood abuse is a key part of what drives Beth Moore.

Oral Roberts's childhood tuberculosis was a key element that drove his ministry. Franklin Graham's struggle growing up with a famous ministry father was a key part of the journey to becoming an evangelist himself. Nancy Alcorn's frustration at the neglect and hurtful treatment of pregnant single women drove her to build a global network of Mercy Ministry homes that counsel, teach and train young mothers.

Many social activists work from a past that motivates them toward change. Some pastors and ministry leaders are particularly focused on ministry to businesspeople because they came out of that background. Many pastors were driven in their younger years by sports.

With some people, their motivation is trauma; with others, it's triumph.

So what's the point? What drives you? Is there a consuming fire that burns within your heart? Is there a desire that can't be quenched? Your passion might be the result of your background, either as a child or an adult; it might be a particular expertise in an unusual area; it might be something you've felt strongly about all your life.

Whatever your driving motivation, it will impact the brand story about you and your ministry. The fact that the pastor of an outreach to bikers was a member of an outlaw motorcycle gang before he became a Christian is a key element in presenting his identity. A career geneticist might begin a nonprofit focused on resolving issues of faith and science. A businessman who is fascinated by a particular area of study might begin a foundation that funds educational programs for decades to come. If you want to minister to Hollywood professionals, although it's not required, a previous career as an actor, producer or other peer is significantly helpful to engage your audience.

There are actually two issues at stake here: *credibility* and *motive*.

Credibility. If you have experience in a particular area of ministry or nonprofit work, it becomes far easier to win support from your potential audience. If you have a passion for sports, movies, church history or psychology, that passion should figure into your branding in some unique way. In the same vein, past trauma might be helpful in ministry to others who have experienced similar struggles. Having a medical background gives you credibility in raising money for a medical outreach to the Third World.

Building your brand story often begins with your past and your purpose.

Motive. I've discovered that a successful and fulfilling life in the nonprofit world comes from years of difficult work, plowing new ground and pioneering where others often fear to tread. During the difficult times, your motive will be a key driving force to keep your momentum moving forward. If Beth Moore's motivation was to be a celebrity, chances are, all the frustrating years she studied and worked in oblivion would have caused her to give up. But because she's driven by her experience of abuse and the potential to help others get through their own trauma, she has the determination to keep going.

One of the reasons I bring up this issue is that staggering numbers of pastors and ministry leaders run away from their past. They make no connection with an experience or an expertise that could help fuel their ministry and provide great credibility with their audience.

In recent years, pastors and ministry leaders have been less afraid to admit past struggles and mistakes, and they've discovered that it often actually strengthens the bond with their partners and supporters.

So ask yourself, *Why am I doing this?* Figure it out, and it will help you discover your brand story.

Ask eight out of ten pastors and ministry leaders why they do what they're doing and you'll get a pat answer like, "I just want to reach people with the gospel." That's nice. But it's the other two pastors and ministry leaders that fascinate me. Of course they want to do the same thing, but they are driven by a passionate connection to the audience either through a dramatic personal experience, a powerful love for a particular cultural group or an intense desire to make a difference. Those two people are the ones who will change the world.

Branding Question #2: Who Are You?

The second question is, *Who exactly are you?* The purpose of this question is to discover what makes you who you are. Do you come from a rich or poor family? Are you an immigrant? Do you have less than a high school education? Do you have a college education or graduate degree? Are you from a distinctive geographic region such as the South? Married or single? Fat or skinny? Handicapped? Tall or short? Conservative or liberal? Do you suffer from Attention Deficit Disorder? The questions could go on, but you get the idea.

Your goal is to discover your DNA, or how you're personally wired. A pastor with a thick Southern accent who was raised by cotton farmers is going to have a different perspective on life than a rich prep-school grad from New England. An evangelist who cut his teeth on inner-city ministry will be different than a rural tent revivalist. A leader with an academic focus will view life differently from a pastor with a ministry to outlaw bikers. A businessman who founds a museum will have a different perspective from a Ph.D. who does the same thing.

I often get resistance when I ask this question, but it's critical information even in today's culture of absorption. If you really delve into your past—your family history and your upbringing—it will reveal a lot about who you are and how you function today. Do you have unresolved issues with your father or mother? If you were abused or abandoned as a child and have never adequately dealt with it, sooner or late it will come up.

In spite of God's saving grace, and even after we've made Jesus Christ the Lord of our life, we often carry baggage from our past. Saved or not, childhood abuse doesn't go away, hurt and pain doesn't necessarily disappear, and our educational or financial limitations are still present. Certainly we have a new Resource to deal with those issues, and the power of God in our lives can transform our circumstances, but salvation isn't necessarily about making obstacles disappear.

A saved *turkey is still a turkey.*

That's why I cringe when religious television programs feature interviews with celebrities who have only recently come to faith. Certainly we're all thrilled that they made that decision, but that doesn't mean they understand how to communicate their newfound faith. I'll admit it does make for interesting television, but on more than one occasion, a new Christian has shocked a national television audience by uttering a profanity or telling an off-color joke, simply because he didn't know any better. He hadn't had time to really learn what the Christian life was all about.

We preach from the pulpit a message about the need for continued growth in our Christian walk, but we often don't deal with it in our own life. That's why, when I'm helping to position a client in the most effective way possible, it's critically important to discover his or her personal issues, both positive and negative.

I wrestle a great deal with how ministry leaders are wired. Certainly God can heal any weakness or negative personality trait, but I've discovered that most people carry deep-seated issues throughout their life. In those cases, we have to learn to work within those limitations or, better yet, use them to our advantage.

How My Weakness Has Become an Advantage

Although I've never been officially diagnosed, most people who know me would agree that I suffer from Attention Deficit Disorder (A.D.D). I'm the king of the short attention span. For years, when people would come into my office for a meeting, my assistant would whisper in their ear, "When his eyes glaze over, the meeting is finished."

In my case, it's a distraction factor. As long as I can remember, I could be distracted by anything, any time. As a preacher's kid who had to sit on the front row every time the church doors were open, I knew the exact number of ceiling tiles in the sanctuary and the number of steps across the stage, and I had mentally traced every design on the altar a million times. As my dad preached, my mind raced, and it still races today.

As a result, I have to close the shutters on my office windows when I write, and I have to turn off my email or else those little messages start calling my name. I've discovered that I'm most productive when I'm trapped. So I always take my laptop on planes, where my distractions are limited and my options are few.

I tried medication once, but we discovered that it masked my creativity and personality almost as if a cloud had descended on my mind, and suddenly I became lethargic, boring and flat. It took away my "spark," and even my long-suffering wife, Kathleen, wanted me off the pills.

In spite of the frustrations and limitations of A.D.D., I've learned to channel my personality in positive directions. I've discovered that I'm gifted at multi-tasking: I'm able to own a production and consulting company for nonprofits, I'm a founding partner in a TV commercial company, I have a regular speaking schedule, I play the piano and I write numerous magazine articles and books. Because I can do many things at once, I'm able to talk on a conference call, answer email and view a client's TV program—all at the same time.

I also discovered that I notice things that others never see. I was driving with a friend across Dallas a few years ago when I remarked about the design of a neon sign far in the distance. It wasn't the sign itself that interested me, but the design the neon lights formed at the angle to our car. My friend remarked how that was a perfect example of something about me he'd noticed before. He would not have seen that particular design in a million years; but probably because of my attention deficit, my eyes were bouncing around all over the place, seeing objects, designs and combinations of images most people would never notice.

Most likely that is the reason I became a television and film director; I can often see things in people, scenes or images that others don't see.

I've learned to take what most people would consider a negative and turn it into a positive. (Which in this case is the reason I'm so skeptical about the various medications people turn to for their A.D.D. children. Even though I'm sure I was a handful for my mother, I wonder how many creative sparks have been extinguished by kids popping pills.)

Life can throw us a lot of curves.

Our childhood, our parents, our physical challenges, our early experiences on the job—all indelibly imprint us with behaviors that are hard to shake. A woman abused as a child, a man whose father told him he'd never amount to much, a person who lives with insecurity—big or small, these things damage our relationships, the quality of our work and our chances for success. But there are three specific personality quirks that can seriously keep people from achieving all they could become in life. I'm not a psychologist, and I don't have all the answers for fixing these problems, but I've discovered that if we can take a frank look at ourselves and at least recognize limiting behaviors, we can get started on the road to freedom.

Traits and Behaviors That Limit Effectiveness

As a pastor or ministry leader, take a hard look at this list of three behaviors, and if you suffer from any of them, stop blaming others and put some effort into making real adjustments. Trust me, everyone else knows about your behavior, so you might as well try to fix it.

1. *Insecurity*

Maybe you felt belittled or unworthy as a child, or feared you would never be good enough. Oddly enough, the real problem with insecurity is that it makes us overbearing. After all, the last thing we want is for people to recognize that we don't know what we're doing! As a result, insecure ministry leaders and executives take charge, assume an arrogant attitude, order others around and become a virtual Nazi in the office. Professional ministry and humanitarian work are breeding grounds for insecure people. After all, many churches are filled with adoring members who can't do enough for the pastor, and they end up feeding an addiction.

I've seen preachers thrive on accolades such as, "Oh pastor, that was such an anointed message." It's tough to keep an even keel when people look to you as God's man or woman. I've seen pastors and ministry leaders with private garages, personal escorts, bodyguards, entourages, and more. It's difficult to stay in a spirit of humility when you're surrounded by the trappings of stardom.

The current rage in many churches is the role of "armor bearer." While the term is a bit out of touch, the concept isn't necessarily a bad one. Based on an assistant who helps a warrior with his armor, in today's churches it's often a personal assistant who carries the pastor's cell phone, Bible or briefcase, helping him or her with schedules, navigating crowds, driving cars, and dealing with other details.

If you need a personal assistant, that's fine. (I have a terrific one.) Some people can be far more productive with the help of an assistant. It allows you to focus on the big picture, while your assistant handles the day-to-day issues. But when someone makes it a "spiritual" thing, I start to get nervous. And when the need turns into a full-blown entourage, it's usually based on insecurity and the need to be noticed.

Remember, if you suffer from insecurity, it's driving people crazy, and the truth is, you actually look the opposite of how you want to appear. People notice, so fix it.

2. *Negativity*

Perhaps the only way some ministry leaders were noticed as a child was pointing out what was wrong with everything. Now they feel it's their job to point out all the ways that ideas or projects won't work. They feel a certain expertise at discovering flaws and criticizing others. I often joke about these people as having the "gift of criticism."

Some people know they don't have original ideas, but at least they can get attention by popping other people's balloons. I've been in leadership meetings with pastors who ripped apart staff members and even family members. The truth is, no one wants to work with a killjoy; after a while, people hate even being around these types of people. Some pastors have almost a split personality—loving and compassionate in the pulpit, but biting and vicious in private.

Objectivity and *negativity* are two different things. Trust me, the flaws in any project will appear soon enough, and encouragement is a rare commodity. Even when you're frustrated with your ministry team, criticism is rarely the answer. We need more ministry leaders who express positive ideas, not negative energy.

3. *Refusing to Listen*

Too many pastors and ministry leaders take the "anointed of God" thing way too seriously. Just because they're called to preach doesn't mean they're above good counsel, advice and constructive criticism. They don't listen to other people because they're usually thinking of what to say next. These leaders have their own ideas, and the last thing they want to hear is something different. The truth is, people can see this behavior a mile away. When you're not really listening, we can spot it in your eyes.

Besides, when you refuse to listen, you're only keeping yourself from wonderful insight and information. One of the greatest skills is to learn the art of listening. When you truly learn to listen, you won't believe what you've been missing.

Can negative traits be changed?

I believe that negative behavior can be changed, but when it is deeply imbedded, it's only through the grace of God and serious counseling that you can get free. Serious personality and behavior traits need to be fully understood to get at the root of *who you are.*

In consultation meetings with a client pastor or ministry leader, we've discovered insights that surprised the client and helped us enormously in our branding work with them. For instance, one pastor who is considered highly experienced and has a very successful television program discovered from his team that his church members considered him aloof, distant and cold. It wasn't behavior he intentionally modeled, but because of the size of his church and the scope of his ministry, cultivating personal relationships was difficult for him. It had become obvious to the people that surrounded him, but not to him. Dealing with 8 people when starting a church in a living room is radically different from growing to 8,000 in an arena-sized sanctuary.

In another case, we discovered a CEO who was so detail-oriented that he was approving light bulb purchases for the company in spite of the fact that he had more than 100 employees. I gently reminded him that his job was to lead, not get bogged down in the day-to-day operations of the ministry.

Others have discovered that their regional accents were so strong that they were difficult to understand in the pulpit, their choice in clothes made people uncomfortable, or a childhood of abuse made it difficult to relate to their own employees. Were these issues obvious? Not to the pastor or executive. Were they important for the organization? Absolutely. Anything that hinders or frustrates the full operation of your gifts and talents is something that should be dealt with as soon as possible.

The Big Picture of How You're Wired

We've spent some time defining negative traits that impact branding. Positive character and personality traits are also a critical part of defining a successful brand. Here are both positive and negative possibilities that you might list about yourself as you work on defining your brand:

Enthusiastic
Controlling
Passive
Loyal
Systematic
Perfectionist
Mature
Sensitive
Visionary
Charismatic
Outgoing
People-oriented

Patient
Passionate
Fun
Decisive
Retrained
Conservative
Liberal
Modest
Withdrawn
Change-oriented
Deliberate
Firm

Opinionated
Tactless
Creative
Quality-driven
Obsessive
Critical
Educated
Timid
Sarcastic
Witty

Consider all the personal qualities that make you human and add them to this list. The question "Who are you?" becomes a vital foundation stone for knowing what you're made of. And don't be so sure that you know all the answers until you get your team in the room with you.

This kind of assessment is similar to professional personality tests available today through psychologists, counselors and business consultants. I would encourage you to explore these types of assessments and other possibilities in a biblically responsible manner. I'm for any proven tool that helps you see an objective view of your strengths and weaknesses, because without an adequate assessment, you'll never discover your true potential.

Branding Question #3: What Are Your Gifts and Talents?

The third question discovers what you're really good at. What were you born to do? A grammar teacher may cringe at my sentence construction, but you get the point.

The key to answering this question is honesty. The question is not "What would you *like* to be good at doing in the future?" It's "What are you good (or gifted) at *now*?" I always recommend a "come to Jesus" meeting with yourself on this one, and if you're working with your team, make sure they are absolutely honest with you.

Here are some of the answers I've received from clients who have described their gifts and talents:

- Preaching
- Teaching
- Writing
- Leading
- Managing
- Singing
- Leading worship
- Technology
- Education
- Business
- Youth ministry
- Missions
- Fund-raising
- Administration
- Team building
- Financial management
- Media ministry
- Intercessory prayer
- Music
- Sports
- Development
- Fitness
- Construction

The list can be long, depending on the particular gifts and talents you may have.

This is where we find out if what you're doing matches your skill set. If you're the senior pastor but you can't preach, there might be a problem. If you're a youth director, but you hate working with kids, we should rethink your brand. If you're a CEO and don't understand finances, we have a challenge.

In most cases, it's not so obvious as those examples. In one case, a leader started out in evangelistic ministry only to encounter serious challenges with fund-raising, managing a ministry, working with a team, and more. Once we explored his personal gifts in relation to the brand, we realized that he was better suited as a writer. In that capacity he didn't have to raise money, manage a team or worry about invitations to preach. Once he left traditional evangelism and focused on writing books, his ministry blossomed.

In another case, a young couple who were in youth ministry in Los Angeles were miserable. They loved young people but just didn't seem suited for the job. I offered to explore their brand through questions like the ones we've just discussed.

We discovered that they were actually wired for missions. Today they manage a growing Christian school in Mexico.

Traditionally, in the Church, we've rightly put enormous emphasis on calling but haven't spent much time connecting that calling to actual gifts and talents. As a result, we have pastors who shouldn't be in the pulpit, youth leaders that teenagers can't relate to and missionaries who are ill equipped and miserable.

Some organizations have developed personal gift inventories and evaluations, and I applaud those resources. They can be exceptional tools for helping believers truly understand how their abilities and spiritual gifts impact their calling. Personality profiles are also helpful resources for revealing personal strengths and weaknesses.

There's no question that God can transcend personal gifts and talents, and He does so on occasion. Sometimes we need to be put in a position where it's clear that our personal abilities cannot accomplish our goal, and we need to rely on God's power and grace. Nehemiah rebuilt the walls of Jerusalem while facing enormous opposition, and yet he knew nothing about fortress design and construction. He was a cupbearer to the king and spent his life doing little more than working in the kitchen. If he had any skill at all, he was probably an expert on wine. But he had a willing heart and was open to learning and to the power of change. In the face of criticism, apathy and threats on his life, he rallied the Jewish people and accomplished something that gave an entire nation hope.

Never close the door on the possibilities that God can accomplish through your life with or without the appropriate skill set. But your job isn't to take the easy way out. You can't sit on the sofa and wait for God when you should be learning, growing and developing your gifts and talents.

Someone once said that if you make stoves, you should be famous among cooks. If you make fishing lures, you should be famous among fishermen. And if you make airplanes, you should be famous among pilots. You can't be all things to all people when it comes to marketing. What do your specific gifts and talents say about the potential audience that could benefit from your particular ministry?

Your real gifts and talents may have nothing to do with your present position.

Forbid the thought, but just because you're a pastor right now doesn't necessarily mean that you have a talent or calling for that job. You may be managing a Christian television studio or network, but perhaps you got the job based on something other than your skill. Although usually motivated by good intentions, family connections have often driven people into jobs and careers that ruined their lives. Never be deluded into thinking that being in your present job means that you're actually qualified for it.

One of the most tragic situations I encounter is when a famous ministry parent pushes his or her son or daughter into the same calling without taking the time to explore the son's or daughter's unique gifts and talents. In some cases, the parent is driven by such ego that he or she would never consider another alternative; but for most, it's a financial consideration: The church or ministry has simply grown so large that the founder feels that a "successor" is the only way to continue the legacy.

I've worked with ministries in which a son felt the burden so powerfully that he completely sublimated his own dreams to copy the ministry of his famous father. As a result, he never discovered his own "brand," and once the father and his financial supporters eventually died, the son had to start building his own unique identity, but by then it was too late.

That's why this branding exercise is so critically important. Our goal is to motivate you to find the right expression for your gifts and talents. You may have been born to write, or you learned to preach in school, or you inherited an uncanny ability to relate to others. Whatever your gifts and talents, identifying them accurately can save you from a life of frustration and failure.

Branding Question #4: What Makes You Different?

Finally, you need to discover what separates you from the pack. In the secular advertising world, this is sometimes referred to as "the unique selling proposition." In other words, what's different and unique about your product compared to the competition?

In a media-driven world, being different is everything. Today, an average grocery store has more than 30,000 items on its shelves. Near the turn of the century, my grandmother's family shopped at a rural grocery store in North Carolina, and choices weren't part of the process. They found one brand of flour, one type of butter and one source of milk.

Today, when my wife, Kathleen, shops at the local grocery store, she faces thousands of choices. On my last visit, I noticed about 12 types of Oreo cookies. Now, even staples like butter, milk, sugar and flour compete for consumers' favor by offering almost endless variations, such as low-fat, skim, flavored, sugar-free, soy. Butter and milk can even come from a wide variety of animals and feature a wide variety of flavors.

Bottled water is my favorite grocery store example of branding. When I was growing up, I always thought water was free (stupid me). But in bottled form, it's not only expensive (bought in bulk it's more expensive than gasoline), but you also can find a wide range of varieties. The question is, outside the obvious choice of flavored, vitamin-enriched or energy-laden water, what's the big difference?

It's *branding*. Sure there may be slight variations in taste because different companies bottle water from different sources. But the real difference is perception. It's not a *content* issue; it's a *style* issue.

It's about the branding.

Kathleen's favorite water is Vos, which scientifically is the same H_2O as Evian, Dasani, Perrier, Arrowhead, Pellegrino, and many others; but the brand couldn't be more different. While other water brands come in plastic bottles in various shapes, Vos water comes in a glass cylinder that forms a perfect tube. It's hip and contemporary with clean lines and a simple design. Not your father's bottled water. (Not that my father has ever touched bottled water.)

With Vos, it's not about the water; it's about the story told by the bottle. Their advertising continues that story of "cool" and "sophistication" so that it connects with the customer.

With bottled water, it's not about the content; it's about the branding.

In the same way, there are a massive number of churches in your city, a multitude of media ministries and a host of preachers and ministry leaders.

What makes you different?

Beyond other churches and ministries, there's even more competition out there within the greater culture. How can you compete with all the entertainment choices, lifestyle options or new digital technologies that struggle to engage the average person's limited discretionary time? You may not have the resources, finances or assets of the competition, but you can tell a better story; and the key to finding that story is discovering what makes you unique and different.

Perhaps it's your unique preaching or teaching style, your writing ability, your personality or an expertise in an unusual area. Being different can mean many things, including perspective, content, skill and delivery.

Perhaps your humanitarian organization does the same thing—say, feeding the hungry—as many other organizations, but you need to find a different way of doing it or do it in a different place.

If your focus is the media, think of an area that isn't covered right now on radio or television. When James Dobson began his radio program years ago, there weren't many programs talking about parenting and family issues. The same was true of other ministries that focused around finances, prophecy or business. It's about pushing creativity to its limits and discovering what it's like to explore life from the perspective of a Bible that starts with "in the beginning, God created."

Branding the Real Thing

Ultimately, successful branding is all about authenticity, because being unique and different doesn't mean fake. Someone once said that *Hollywood does an incredible job of making fake things look real, and Christians do an incredible job of making real things look fake.* In our efforts to relate to the culture, churches and ministries often go over the top and end up conveying a message that's obviously dishonest and far from authentic.

I'm told that I was born with the gift of saying what everyone else in the room is thinking. Whether or not it gets me in trouble, I often feel compelled to talk about the elephant in the room that everyone else sees but ignores. That's why this issue of authenticity is so important to me. I was born with a very sensitive B.S. button, and anytime a church or ministry presents an advertisement, website, TV program or other presentation that smacks of insincerity, my button lights up.

Apparently, that genetic trait was passed on to my youngest daughter, Bailey. For years, I've been asked to judge various film and video festivals, many of which were Christian events. When Bailey was a little girl, I would bring her in whenever I had to judge a children's programming category. After all, it was TV programming designed for her age group, so I was curious about her reaction.

Most of the time, it was tough to keep her in the room. Even as a young child, she was quick to point out how cheesy and cornball most of the programs were, and I would often use her reaction as a factor in my judging. Kids tell you the truth, and I wish more Christians who create kid's programming used children as critics.

One major national chain of toy stores has created an advisory panel of 10-year-olds to help them make buying decisions. Churches and ministries involved in creating kid's programs should consider the brilliance of that idea.

On my blog, I've done a number of informal surveys over the years to gauge the reaction of the culture to religious media. In most cases, the issue of authenticity is at the top of the list. Historically, audiences have had trouble relating to Christians in media because although they seem earnest, they don't really seem sincere. So we have to understand the critical importance of honesty, reality and authenticity when we create a brand.

Ultimately, a significant part of being different is being honest about who you are and how you are perceived.

Jesus Junk

One of the most damaging attacks on our authenticity happens when media ministries offer kitsch on television in exchange for donations. My alarm goes off at 5:50 sharp every morning, so I drag myself out of bed and head to the garage where I keep my exercise equipment and treadmill. While working out, I often turn on various TV channels to keep track of the early morning round of TV evangelists. I've been producing television programming for more than 30 years now, and I'm still amazed and often shocked at the junk some evangelists pitch on television.

Vials of anointing oil and "miracle water" are still big, as well as prayer cloths, miracle seeds, Scripture key chains, plastic statues of Jesus, and gimmicks of all kinds. I prefer to call it "Jesus Junk." One TV prophet will even give you a "personal prophecy" (once you call and give him your credit card number).

How did we come to this? How has the historic Christian faith that defeated the Roman empire, transformed nations, inspired the greatest art, music and science in the Western world stooped to offering cheap trinkets and religious trash?

The truth is, we've created a generation of Christians who are looking for a magic bullet. That's why people travel thousands of miles from conference to conference just to "get a word," find "fresh oil," "get the glory" or "catch their blessing." The truth is, they're looking for the easy way out.

It's interesting that after World War II, we experienced an age of virtual miracles in this country. We had amazing pre-fab housing, miracle drugs, fast food, space age appliances and instant satisfaction. And it changed everyone. I had an uncle who experienced three heart attacks but refused to exercise or eat right. He was waiting on a miracle drug to solve his health problems. He died still waiting.

It's no wonder that in such a marvelous era, "miracle ministries" were born. Men and women like Oral Roberts, William Branham, Kathryn Kuhlman, Jack Coe and others exploded on the scene with amazing success. They ignited a new passion for the supernatural and the gifts of the Spirit.

But now, 50-plus years later, the pendulum has swung so far that we've become addicted to the feeling. We've forgotten how difficult living the Christian life can be, and in our pursuit of prosperity and a nice Mercedes, we've lost touch with the fact that the apostle Paul rotted in prison. And what about Peter's horrific upside-down crucifixion? And William Tyndale being strangled and burned at the stake for giving us the remarkable gift of the English Bible?

Yes, God calls us to live in victory, but real triumph comes from doing battle in the difficult trenches of life. Frankly, in this post-Christian culture, it's not going to get easier. Research indicates that millions profess Christianity but know remarkably little about the basic principles of the faith. As a result, they think *The Da Vinci Code* is true, and they wonder if the "gospel" of Judas should be included in the Scriptures.

The book of Acts records that when handkerchiefs that touched Paul were taken to the sick, they were healed. But Paul didn't have the handkerchiefs mass-marketed and used for a fund-raising scheme. God prospers people, but the Christian faith isn't about new cars, chasing a blessing or getting a word. It's about taking up our cross. It's about making the time to study God's Word.

As the apostle Paul said:

> I want to know Christ and the power of his resurrection and the fellowship of sharing in his sufferings, becoming like him in his death, and so, somehow, to attain to the resurrection from the dead (Phil. 3:10-11).

I believe that the damage done to the Christian faith by hucksters is incalculable. I also believe that enormous damage can be done by people with the best of intentions—by people who love God and are struggling to present His message to the world. The problem happens when we try so hard that we lose our authenticity. "Meaning well" doesn't make up for the public's perception of insincerity.

Finding your honest voice in the middle of the media madness is absolutely critical. You don't want to try to duplicate what some other successful ministry leader has done. You need to be absolutely honest about what distinguishes you from the pack. I believe that God made everyone unique, and that's why finding your unique combination of gifts and talents is the key to creating your unique voice.

CHAPTER SIX

THE RIGHT BRANDING TOOLS

Don't bring a knife to a gunfight.
ANONYMOUS

That's a lesson for anybody selling anything—a hamburger, a candidate, or eternal life. It's the connection that counts.
DOUGLAS B. SOSNICK, MATTHEW J. DOWD AND RON FOURNIER, *APPLEBEE'S AMERICA*[1]

Nearly every week churches and ministries send copies of their media programs to our office to ask us for advice. *How can we produce our program more effectively? Can you design a new logo for us? Can you help us with our lighting? What about our editing?* Usually the questions come from pastors or ministry leaders frustrated about the poor quality of their television outreach.

The truth is, a significant number of churches and ministries produce very poor programming without realizing that the lack of quality is a huge obstacle to viewers. In the early days of television, people were fascinated that they could see a program at all. "Snow," poor audio or bad lighting didn't bother them, because the new medium was such a marvel.

But in a high-definition world, with multiple channels, the competition is so great with most cable or satellite television systems that the slightest problem with quality causes viewers to find another program. That's why choosing the right medium for your message—and using the right tools—

is a key part of the branding puzzle.

Many of the programs sent to my office feature great preaching and teaching. But I won't watch if the lighting, camera work, directing or editing makes the viewing experience miserable. Many potential breakthrough talents in ministry today are terribly obscured because they preach their message through the wrong medium or with faulty tools.

Part of Joel Osteen's brand is his quality of production. His weekly program looks so good that it creates a buzz of its own. I've heard many people talk about the show, and the first thing they usually mention is the production quality of the program. Certainly compared to other programs on Christian television, it looks fantastic.

Quality Versus Response

One of the most asked questions I receive is, "Once I create a strong brand, will producing programs, especially commercial spots and product offers with higher production quality, get a higher response?"

There's no real way to know. In my experience the results have been around 50/50. Sometimes the higher quality cuts through the television clutter and connects with the audience, causing them to respond. But at other times, a poorly produced version gets the same and sometimes better response.

From time to time, I've seen ministries create poorly produced programs that still get a terrific response. Later, when they have the money and they update the program to a higher level of professionalism and quality, the response actually drops.

After producing programming for more than three decades, one thing I've learned is that I'll never figure out the TV audience. In spite of marketing tools, research and sophisticated production techniques, sometimes there is no discernible reason that people connect with a certain type of program or product.

On the other hand, I've also discovered that if you want to keep an audience for the long haul, quality is the only way to go.

A higher quality production might not generate a better response at the moment, but it will impact the overall perception of your ministry.

The key reason to produce at the highest and most contemporary level possible is that you're creating a long-term perception in the eyes of your audience. Certainly, a single product or commercial may resonate with the audience, causing them to respond regardless of the production quality. But there's no question that over the long haul, quality always wins out. Plus, a new generation is watching that is more media savvy than ever and tuned into quality. If you want to make an impression with them, badly written, produced or directed programs simply won't cut it.

It's a matter of the brand story you want to leave in the mind of your audience, your church members or your supporters. Remember our original question in the introduction:

What do people think of when they think of you?

So, what do great communicators know about their tools that others don't?

1. The Medium Is the Message

The first time I encountered the subject of "mass communication studies" was as a college freshman in the fall of 1972. At that time, the writings and lectures of Canadian academic and writer Marshall McLuhan were all the rage on college campuses, and our professor was one of his most ardent disciples. By all accounts, McLuhan was brilliant. He was fluent in seven languages, held a Ph.D. from Cambridge in English Literature and received at least 10 honorary doctorates in his lifetime.

In 1959, in the middle of great controversy and hype about the potential of "educational television," he was appointed as director of the National Association of Educational Broadcasters' Media Project, producing statements such as, "Television is teaching all the time. It does more educating than all the schools and all the institutions of higher learning."

McLuhan's *The Gutenberg Galaxy* appeared in 1962, followed by *The Making of Typographic Man* in 1962, *Understanding Media* in 1964, *The Medium Is the Message* in 1967, and *War & Peace in the Global Village* in 1968. He generally wrote his books as collages of short statements or interviews, and he made numerous media appearances, including a spot in Woody Allen's 1977 comedy *Annie Hall.*

But it was his seminal book *Understanding Media: The Extensions of Man* that was regarded as the holy grail of culture studies. He coined the terms "Global Village" and "Age of Information" long before the Internet, and his work has inspired some of the greatest media pioneers of our time.

I had no idea during those years that McLuhan was actually a devout Catholic, and it was his faith that drove much of his work on the media frontier. Back in the early seventies, he believed that centralized Christianity was losing its power, and he predicted the loose-networked movement of independent churches—even mega-churches—long before most people considered the possibility.

The most powerful of McLuhan's pronouncements was the statement that the medium is the message. In other words, the medium we choose to deliver a message has a significant impact on the message itself. In the church, we often say that the message never changes, but the method or medium does. I've heard that phrase over and over again as a clarion call to continually embrace technology and new media in an effort to keep the gospel message alive in the culture.

It sounds good, but if McLuhan is right, it's not true at all. Perhaps the most significant expression of this thinking is his statement, "The content or message of any particular medium has about as much importance as the stenciling on the casing of an atomic bomb." He felt that the medium used to deliver the message is actually far more important than the message itself.

That's pretty tough, but worth serious consideration.

Each time technology develops a new medium, it's not simply an extension of the last, it's far more—it's a completely new and different entity.

Program writers, directors and producers found this out during the early days between the transition from radio to television. When television was first invented, most dramatic scripts were simply radio dramas with pictures. In other words, there wasn't much visual action; directors just shot actors standing around talking to each other. It was flat and lifeless, and the audience wasn't impressed.

That's when someone finally recognized that television was something altogether new. That realization paved the way for what we now call "The Golden Years of Television." That was the period roughly from 1949 to 1960 that is still considered one of the greatest eras of television programming.

In the book *Amusing Ourselves to Death*, media critic Neil Postman discusses the impact that form has over content:

> To take a simple example of what this means, consider the primitive technology of smoke signals. While I do not know exactly what content was once carried in the smoke signals of American Indians, I can safely guess that it did not include philosophical argument. Puffs of smoke are insufficiently complex to express ideas on the nature of existence, and even if they were not, a Cherokee philosopher would run short of either wood or blankets long before he reached his second axiom. You cannot use smoke to do philosophy. Its form excludes the content.[2]

Would Jesus Have Left the Dead Sea Videotapes?

In 1977, British journalist Malcolm Muggeridge echoed McLuhan and Postman when he wrote *Christ and the Media*. His purpose was to examine whether or not Jesus, had He been born in the present day, would have left the Dead Sea Videotapes rather than the Dead Sea Scrolls. Muggeridge was very careful to point out that directing, shooting, lighting and editing techniques can be so manipulated that television is inherently a lie.

He speaks from experience, recounting a remarkable story:

> The most horrifying example I know of the camera's power and authority, which will surely be in the history books as an example of the degradation our servitude to it can involve, occurred in Nigeria at the time of the Biafran War. A prisoner was to be executed by a firing squad, and the cameras turned up in force to

> photograph and film the scene. Just as the command to fire was about to the given, one of the cameramen shouted "Cut!"; his battery had gone dead and needed to be replaced. Until this was done, the execution stood suspended. Then, with his battery working again, he shouted "Action!", and bang, bang, the prisoner fell to the ground, his death duly recorded, to be shown in millions of sitting rooms throughout the so-called civilized world. Some future historian may speculate as to where lay the greatest barbarism, on the part of the viewers, the executioners, or the camera. I think myself that he would plump for the cameras.[3]

Muggeridge admits that we shouldn't throw out technology altogether, but he does give a caution that's worth considering:

> It's very nearly impossible to tell the truth in television, but you can try very hard. As far as the word is concerned, spoken or written, it has been used, and continues to be used, for purposes of deception, and for evil purposes like pornography. This is absolutely true. But, you see, a word comes from a man. Putting it in its simplest terms, if I write a novel, signed by my name, I am saying these are my thoughts, these are my views, these are my impressions, and the response of the reader is according. If you set up a camera and take a film, that is not considered to be anybody's views; that is reality, and, of course, it is much more fantasy than the words. Supposing there had been a film made of the life of our Lord. Do you think that that would have stirred men as the Gospels have?[4]

I respect Muggeridge's views because of his credentials as a journalist and Christian. He presents us a balance but also gives us reasons for great caution as well. As a journalist of his era, he was a print man, no question, and found the transition to film and video challenging at best.

He once wrote about a story by Soviet labor camp survivor Alexander Solzhenitsyn, about a desperate man in the bunk above his who "used to climb up into it in the evening, and take old, much-folded pieces of paper out of his pocket, and read them with evident satisfaction. It turned out that they had passages from the Gospels scribbled on them, which were his solace and joy in that terrible place. He would not, I feel sure, have been similarly comforted and edified by re-runs of old footage of religious TV programs."[5]

The Da Vinci Disconnect

I was reminded of the disconnect and frustration of the medium in 2006 when the movie *The Da Vinci Code* was about to hit movie screens across North America. In the middle of a huge controversy about the impact of the film, I decided to jump into the conversation. After posting a number of articles on my blog at philcooke.com detailing my thoughts on how Christians should respond to the film, the posts were picked up by the producers of news talk shows on MSNBC, CNBC, and CNN. As a result, I was invited to be a guest with hosts Joe Scarborough and Paula Zahn. We normally think of these types of cable shows as legitimate news programs, sparking debate and discussion on contemporary issues, but I soon discovered the exasperating limitations.

Because of my busy travel schedule, I was usually asked to come to a local TV station or news affiliate in whatever city I was in so that they could connect to me live via satellite for the interview. After arriving, I would be ushered into a small black room with a single TV camera pointed at my chair. No TV monitors were in the room, so I couldn't actually see the program host or the other guest against whom I might be debating.

In addition, I rarely even knew what points would be discussed, or the experts I might be up against. The host or hostess completely controlled the interview, and without being able to see anyone, I was totally dependent on the earpiece that connected me to the program's audio track.

The most difficult part to navigate was that I had no idea how many times I could respond to an issue, and I never knew if my current comment was my last. So the actual development of a line of thought was impossible, and the best I could hope for was a fragment or short statement that made sense. Worse, I occasionally would have to confront a belligerent guest, so anything I said had to be timed between his or her tirades.

I've been featured on Paula Zahn's program multiple times, and she's a brilliant and gracious journalist. When I'm on the air, we're like friends, but I've never actually met her or spoken one word to her outside my actual time live on the broadcast.

Such is the nature of the medium and the resulting impact on political and cultural discourse.

Do we toss out technology? No. But McLuhan, Postman and Muggeridge teach us that we can't be too careful in how we present an eternal message on a temporal medium. The medium does indeed impact the message.

2. Choose the Right Medium

When William Tyndale translated the Bible into English in the sixteenth century, it changed the course of history. And yet, it would have made far less impact if he hadn't understood the power of the right medium.

Due to the limitations of printing, most books were very large and heavy. Think of the old twenty-pound family Bible you might have grown up with and you'll get the idea. They were also bound in leather, which made owning books too expensive for most people. As a result, only scholars and the very rich read books on a regular basis.

Tyndale knew that for his translation to have impact, it would have to be read by thousands of people, so he published his English New Testament in a smaller-sized version that anyone could carry around in his pocket. It was the first time a Bible had been printed in such small dimensions, and it became a sensation. During Tyndale's lifetime, it was illegal to own a Bible in the English language, so the convenience of its size made it easy to hide. It wasn't long before thousands of these translations were being published and read secretly throughout the British Isles.

Because Tyndale understood the power of the right medium, his impact cannot be measured.

With modern media, there's an old quote that says it all: *He has a face for radio.* In a media-driven culture, looks matter, and unless you have other reasons to work in a visual medium, never forget the impact that radio can have in the culture. Christian and talk radio is huge business; it's much less expensive than television. And now with satellite and Internet radio, its influence is being felt in other places as well.

But it's not just about looks. What about your message works particularly well on television? Would it be better as a podcast on the Web, a video clip on the church website or a periodic DVD special that you mail to homes? Television certainly gets a lot of attention, but increasingly, it's not the only game in town.

Today the number of video downloads from sites like Youtube.com compete with the audience numbers of prime-time television networks. A line has clearly been crossed, and there's a significant audience out there that most churches, ministries and nonprofits know little or nothing about.

Even if you choose television as your medium, a weekly 30-minute program may not be the answer. I had one client in the Midwest who was a pastor with a heart to reach men. Realizing that another 30-minute program wouldn't help separate him from the ministry pack, he started producing 30-*second* spots and used them to sponsor the local sports report on a television network affiliate station in his community. As a result, he's reaching more men during those 30-second breaks than all the full-length Christian programs in his market combined. He writes the spots around male-oriented subjects and speaks into the lives of thousands of men every night during the network news.

It's a perfect example of thinking differently and being innovative in a competitive market.

Cultural Sensitivity

The medium used is largely dependent on the cultural setting. Think of how TV is viewed in the United States versus a country like China, where broadcasting is extremely regulated. In the Middle East, satellite dishes litter rooftops, even in countries where watching the wrong networks can result in imprisonment. Under those constraints, media use takes on a completely different character.

While teaching in Russia a few years ago, I was dismayed to find so many American TV evangelists broadcasting the same programs throughout Eastern Europe as they broadcast in Cleveland or Toledo. I urge faith-based programmers to understand that audiences in China, Iraq or the Sudan don't watch their program through the same lens as those in Los Angeles or Dallas.

When youth network MTV exploded globally a number of years ago, one of the first strategies they implemented was to open local bureaus in major countries around the world. They knew that the key to success was cultural sensitivity, so they focused MTV-India on local musicians and artists and did the same in various geographic regions throughout the world. Today, MTV's programming is different in different countries, and as a result, their global fan base is staggering.

One of the few Christian TV networks to follow that example is the SAT-7 Network in the Middle East. Because they are broadcasting via satellite primarily to Arab audiences in the Middle East and North Africa, they rely primarily on local programming that resonates with the interests and needs of their audience.

Many years ago, I was filming in the Amazon rain forest. After taking a commercial flight to the center of Brazil, chartering a light plane to go deeper into the jungle and negotiating a river freighter to take us two more days upriver, we finally moved our equipment to canoes for the last day's journey near the headwaters of the legendary river. It wouldn't be a stretch to say we were about as far from civilization as you could imagine.

Our task was to film a remote Brazilian tribe, but when we arrived in the village, it was deserted. There were six crude thatched huts in the clearing, and we walked carefully from hut to hut looking for any sign of life. When we finally came to the last shelter, to our shock and surprise, we discovered that all the villagers were crammed into the small hut, crowded around a beat-up black-and-white TV set powered by an ancient car battery.

They were watching a static-filled broadcast from who knows where of the American television series *Dallas.* I stood there in stunned amazement, wondering what these isolated tribesmen thought of J. R. and Sue Ellen and how that knowledge would potentially screw up their perceptions and culture for years to come.

The medium impacts the message, and the medium is viewed differently in diverse locations and cultures. Choosing the right medium for the message and the right medium for the audience is critical. For whatever situation, we need to be extremely careful in the media we select.

3. Get the Right Advice

One of the great frustrations of my career has been seeing great churches and religious organizations crippled because of the wrong advice. Advancing technology has caused the price of audio and video equipment to tumble dramatically during the last 30 years, but don't be fooled–creating a major national media outreach is still an expensive proposition.

Today, outsourcing is all the rage in corporate America. The theory behind the practice is worth thinking about: If there is some aspect of your business that you don't do well, then outsource it to someone who does. For instance, a corporation that builds computers might not be so strong at strategic planning; or a company that manufactures sports equipment probably doesn't understand marketing and public relations. So they find consultants with experience and success in those areas to give them advice, training and expertise.

Could churches, ministries and other Christian organizations benefit from the concept?

Absolutely.

Although our mandate for reaching the lost couldn't be simpler, the various ways available to accomplish that mandate couldn't be more complex. Today, churches and ministries routinely use new technology, the media, branding, marketing strategies, leadership training and other tools to make their outreaches, educational programs and ministries more effective.

That's why thousands of churches and parachurch ministries around the world use consultants (experts in particular fields) to help them understand and implement their outreaches more effectively. Consultants are available in areas such as Christian education, computer technology, TV and radio production, media, strategic planning, leadership, branding, marketing and advertising, and more; and they can make a real difference in raising the level of competence for your staff members, employees and leaders.

I've observed so many churches and ministries, as well as Christian media organizations, that use consultants in the wrong ways. So I've created a list of the 10 biggest mistakes and misperceptions in regard to outsourcing. Perhaps this list will change your thinking about consultants and give you some innovative ideas about how they can positively impact your organization and mission.

Mistake #1: Assume That You Don't Need a Consultant

I sat next to a corporate management consultant on a flight who said, "Today, corporate America understands the power of using consultants, and I'm busier than ever. The single most important role a consultant can play is to provide a fresh perspective; companies are willing to pay me a lot of money to do just that." Leadership expert John Maxwell calls it "fresh eyes." Everyone needs someone from the outside to bring a new perspective, valuable experience and cutting-edge thinking to their situation. If you're not using outside sources, especially in areas like the media, TV and radio production; strategic planning; advertising, marketing and direct mail, then you're missing an incredible resource for new and beneficial ideas, principles and techniques. If the most successful companies in America use consultants, perhaps you should consider using them as well.

Mistake #2: Don't Check the Consultant's Track Record

When you hire a consultant, make sure you've hired the right one. Ask for a client list and check those references ahead of time. The best consultants have a great track record, and you can tell from past clients if they have what it takes to impact your church or ministry. Whatever you do, don't just take the consultant's word for it. View their demo reel, client list, portfolio, spreadsheets or other information that documents past successes. Even more important, call their former clients and ask about working with the consultant you are considering.

Mistake #3: Never Give a Consultant Access to the Top Person in the Organization

I know a ministry that recently brought in a direct-mail consultant but never gave him access to the ministry leader. In spite of the fact that the consultant was helping write and edit letters, magazine articles and other materials that needed to express the ministry leader's vision and calling, he never had an opportunity to actually meet and talk with him. Anyone responsible for expressing the pastor or ministry leader's vision through television, radio, print or the Internet desperately needs face time with the boss. If the pastor or ministry or corporate leader is too busy or "too important" to make time for the people who act as his or her gatekeepers to millions of potential partners, viewers and listeners, then his or her priorities are way out of whack.

Mistake #4: Have Middle Managers Criticize the Consultant's Recommendations

If your in-house management team could have solved the problem, you wouldn't have needed to bring in a consultant in the first place. Over and over, I see Christian organizations hire outside experts to help reshape different aspects of ministry outreaches, but the consultants are constantly being micromanaged, evaluated or critiqued by less-experienced in-house managers. Leave the consultant alone long enough to produce results! Certainly don't let him take over the ministry or work without guidelines or supervision. But don't dilute his or her work by allowing your managers to meddle with it.

Mistake #5: Nickel and Dime Your Consultants

Don't hire a consultant and then financially tie his or her hands, especially if the consultant is getting good results. Of course you don't have an unlimited bank account, but sit down with your consultant ahead of time, create an appropriate budget and then let them work inside that framework. The most successful consultants can be expensive, but they know what they're doing and are worth every penny. In fact, beware of consultants who sell themselves too cheaply. Let the good ones have the tools and resources they need to make your company or ministry successful.

Mistake #6: Be Afraid the Consultant Will Take Over

Most consultants work with numerous clients, travel a great deal, set their own hours and run their own business—what a great life! Why in the world would they want to take over your ministry? Actually, nothing could be farther from the truth. The best consultants specialize in areas like media, TV or radio production, fund-raising, employee training, strategic planning, information technology, branding and marketing. They aren't the least bit interested in dealing with personnel issues, correspondence, shipping or other general ministry areas. Their greatest joy is to be wildly successful in the area they were hired to fix, not hijack your organization.

Mistake #7: Don't Take the Consultant Seriously

I've never understood churches and ministries that hire consultants and then don't listen to them. I think this must come from insecurity, inexperience or, in a few cases, a raging ego. The best consultants are people that can transform your ministry and take you to the next level. If you've hired the right person or company, they come to you after working with some of the most successful churches, ministries and organizations in America. Not listening to that type of expertise is like a football team never listening to a winning coach. Don't want to listen? Then don't hire a consultant to begin with.

Mistake #8: If the Consultant Makes a Mistake, Get Rid of Him or Her

I actually like consultants to make mistakes. It means they are trying new things, over-reaching and pushing the limits. Give your consultant room to present ideas that you might not like or don't think would work. Give them a little latitude and they'll pay you back in spades with creative work, innovative ideas and, most of all, results. When they do make a mistake or present an idea or project you don't like, sit down and discuss it at length—what you liked and didn't like, and let them defend their thinking. Often, their motives and reasons are sound and have been used successfully elsewhere.

Mistake #9: Don't Recommend the Consultant to Others

A regular joke in the world of consulting is that every client wants to think they're the only client the consultant has. But remember, the more clients your consultant works with, the wider range of experience, data and ideas he or she brings to your table. Don't hog a good consultant; after all, we're all on the same team. Help your church and ministry friends by sharing good consultants and expanding their client base. Although good consultants keep their client-specific information and data from other organizations highly confidential, their experiences from other ministries will only help you.

Mistake #10: Only Use Consultants for Short-term Projects
In the secular world, client-consultant relationships work for years, and even decades. In television production, for instance, it might take years to build or reshape your television outreach, especially at a national level. Training a crew, buying the right equipment, selecting the best TV stations and networks, building a fund-raising program, developing a long-term media strategy, branding your program, advertising and promotion, graphic design, exploring international media opportunities, and more, take time. Sometimes a consultant can come in and fix something right away, but that's the exception rather than the rule. Look for a consultant who can provide a long-term plan for helping you achieve your goals, and make sure he has the staff, resources and tools for staying with you for the long haul to take your church or ministry to the far reaches of success and effectiveness.

Ask the Right Questions

Here are some important questions about the tools you're using:

- What *traditional* media are you currently using (film, TV, print, radio)?
- What *digital* media tools are you currently using (website, blogs, video blogs, podcasting, streaming media, online communities, social networking)?
- Based on the evidence, what medium delivers your message most effectively?
- What are your media frustrations?
- What are your media opportunities?
- Why do you want to use the media? (What do you hope can be accomplished?)

The Branded Building

One area that a handful of pastors and ministry leaders have maximized is the concept of using architecture to impact the brand. Harvest Church in Riverside, California, has created a public meeting place that looks like a cross between Barnes & Noble, Starbucks, and the city square. You can have lunch, buy a book or CD, drink gourmet coffee or sit in the California sun and relax. It has become so popular that people who would never darken the door of the church on Sunday gladly drop in during the week for lunch. The hip and contemporary design welcomes visitors, and the practicality makes them feel at home.

Mega-churches in recent years have taken a lot of flak for building a coffee bar in the lobby or expanded restaurants and shops; but the truth is, these churches understand the importance of building community as part of the brand. It makes a particular impact among young people, who are trying to initiate connections of their own and are looking for places to meet.

Douglas B. Sosnick, Matthew J. Dowd and Ron Fournier relate their conversation with Starbucks founder Howard Schultz in their book *Applebee's America*, as he described how that company discovered the power of community:

> The desire for atmosphere and camaraderie was most intense among people in their twenties who had grown up with no safe place to hang out other than shopping malls, Schultz told us in 2006. As young adults, some found bars too noisy and threatening for companionship. So they hung out in cars and coffee bars. Other trends of the 1990s helped Starbucks, including the growing number of people who worked from home and used coffee shops as a second office. It helped that the

> Internet was becoming a part of the culture at the same time that Schultz was making Starbucks part of it too. Wireless access to the Internet helped make coffee shops a Third Place. "We have evolved and taken advantage of changes in the way people work and how they live in their homes, and, most of all, the fact that people are very hungry for human contact," Schultz told us. "I think it's a new phenomenon. I think if you kind of get underneath the rise in technology and the way people use personal electronic devices, it has become a secular way in which people act, and that has led to people's desires to have some degree of human contact during the day, and Starbucks has definitely benefited from that."[6]

Notice how many areas Schultz reacted and connected to, because he was always aware of the changes in the culture. He first recognized the need for *place*. So he built a company that didn't just sell a product but also created a safe and comfortable place where people found community. He used architecture as the starting point of building the brand.

Second, he saw the *rise in home-based workers*, so he made the shops a functional place to work. Third, as he watched *the rise in the Internet's popularity*, he made wireless access a priority. Finally, he recognized the need in people's lives for a "Third Place." That's the place you want to be after home and work. It's the Holy Grail of many retailers, who want to capture your time beyond living and working. As a boy growing up in the South, my Third Place was church. We had activities of all kinds throughout the week, because it was a real focal point for the community. The church lost that position beginning in the sixties, but now, pastors are seeing the possibilities of reclaiming that spot in people's lives.

Because Howard Schultz was aware of these changes happening in the culture, he responded with the Starbucks brand and accommodated each of these needs, making the chain of coffee shops the most popular in the world. We don't have to be technology slaves, but we do need to see the changes happening in the culture and recognize how we can respond with our brand.

Branding extends even into the details of the building. Starbucks selected round tables because studies indicated that a single person sitting at a square table makes them look and feel more alone. They also discovered that round tables made the coffee shop flow more from a design point of view. Because a sense of community is important for Starbucks, anything that made people feel alone and separated had to be eliminated or at least toned down to a minimum.

The right tools are the gateway to expressing your brand identity to the world. Whether you use church bulletins, highway billboards, websites, radio, television, podcasting, architecture or something else, using the wrong tools or using them ineffectively will blur your story and contaminate your identity. Create a clear vision for your audience and express that vision from the highest quality launching pad possible.

A great brand will always be hurt by poor communication; and without the right tools, you'll never reach your largest potential audience.

The Power of "Buzz"

In the religious community, we often forget the single greatest result of powerful branding: word of mouth advertising, or "buzz." It could be argued that Joel Osteen sold millions of copies of his book *Your Best Life Now* because of the remarkable success of his weekly television program. TV ratings services report that he's the most watched inspirational program on television, with more than a million viewers each week. In addition, Joel regularly preaches around the country in massive arenas that hold thousands of people in standing-room-only crowds. The meetings have been so successful that the largest arenas have required that Joel's ministry sell tickets in order to control the throngs willing to stand in line for hours just to get a seat. As a result of that national promotion, his books sell in significant numbers.

Joel's momentum is amazing.

I talked with Joel recently about his podcast on iTunes. In just a matter of months, it rose to number nine nationally on the iTunes site. That's the power of momentum in action. We discussed that he doesn't charge customers for the podcast, but it has enormous value because of ubiquity—the fact of being everywhere. In the world of branding, being everywhere is gold. His TV program, his books, his live events, his website and now his podcast give him a platform in multiple arenas for his audience to enjoy, and that combined momentum of multiple locations extends the power of his brand.

Joyce Meyer is no different. Her daily television program is a huge success and, like Joel, she takes her ministry to the road and fills auditoriums and arenas across the country each month. Her bestsellers *Battlefield of the Mind* and *Approval Addiction* are driven in large part by her success on television.

If You Don't Have Mass Media on Your Side

What about Rick Warren's book *The Purpose Driven Life*? Rick doesn't have a television program, and he doesn't do major arena events on a regular basis.

What drove his book to be the biggest selling hardback of all time?

Many would point to his pastors' network and his regular email correspondence with thousands of church leaders. But he has built that network without national radio, TV or even print promotion. His success is an example of the power of word of mouth advertising. People telling other people about your product, church or organization is a powerful tool.

We live in an age of *influencers*, with some researchers saying that at least 1 out of every 10 people is someone the other 9 ask for advice on any number of issues, from restaurants, movies, cars, shopping, churches, and more.

After all, we're drowning in information, and people are looking for answers they can trust. As of this writing, in America there are:

- More than 13,000 radio stations
- More than 1,300 TV stations
- More than 18,000 magazines
- More than 390 full cable networks
- Hundreds more pay-per-view channels
- Tens of millions of websites and online blogs

In Los Angeles alone, between broadcast stations, cable and pay-per-view, I have nearly 500 channels coming into my home. Plus, with two daughters and their friends around, DVD rentals arrive almost daily.

If my wife, Kathleen, has an addiction, it's to magazine subscriptions. She's a sucker for every school kid who drops by selling subscriptions (please don't let the word out), and as a result, we have numerous piles of magazines lined up throughout the house. I take as many magazines as I can cram into a large bag on trips just to catch up.

My weakness is books. I've inherited that from my father, so maybe I have an excuse. But my library is getting into the thousands with no sign of letting up, and I have stacks of unread books just waiting for me to attack.

> *Information is not knowledge.*
>
> **ALBERT EINSTEIN**

We're surrounded by more and more information, and like lost tourists in unknown territory, we desperately need a guide. We always thought the digital revolution would help us leave our shackles of ignorance behind, but now more than ever we've become slaves to technology. Who can possibly make an intelligent choice when so much is thrown at us each day?

In a world of media clutter, who can you trust?

Your friends.

That's why friends sharing the news about your church, ministry or nonprofit is so important.

Research indicates that the single most trusted source for guidance on any number of important issues is another person. Personal relationships help people connect to church, medical services, entertainment, products and a multitude of other important issues.

Taking your message directly to the people is a key part of successful branding. When Toyota wanted to market their new Scion automobile to the Gen Y crowd, instead of massive national advertising, they selectively put a number of the cars on major college campuses across the country. No advertising, no salespeople, no brochures, nothing.

Seeing the cars sitting in parking lots without fanfare or promotion intrigued these kids who had grown up distrustful of regular advertising. So instead of the traditional method of flooding the market with advertising and promotion, Toyota kept the cool factor alive by leaking information out gradually and allowing student influencers to talk it up.

Throughout Malcolm Gladwell's book *The Tipping Point: How Little Things Can Make a Big Difference*, he cites numerous examples of strategic marketing where companies let the influencers guide the conversation with friends and coworkers. Some give out free samples of products to people they know will talk it up. Others stage parties or other events and invite people who will use their influence to promote the product or service. Others focus on returning customers, who feel like part of an insider club and eagerly share this new product with friends and coworkers.

The buzz approach helps in two ways. First, it's perfect if you have a limited budget (and what church, ministry or nonprofit doesn't?). Second, it gives the product credibility, since it's being recommended by a trusted friend.

I'm convinced that's why personal testimonies work so well in the media. In our experience with producing infomercials and direct-response advertising, the phones light up after a personal testimony about the product or organization. We've discovered that a program host or hostess can talk about a product until they're blue in the face, but when the viewer actually sees John Q. Public talking about how the product has changed his life, he apparently thinks, "If it works for him, maybe it will work for me."

Hearing from another person is critical, so in your branding efforts, include testimonies so that your audience can hear from real people how the product or organization has impacted them.

Ultimately, it's about trust. People are growing ever more skeptical about what they're hearing on television or from politicians. But when they hear it from a friend, something rings true.

This is especially true for a younger generation that grew up with advertising. Today's teenagers have been pitched everything and are naturally far more skeptical than any other generation in history. They've seen the cons, heard the trash and read the spam. What they see in the media makes them wary, so they naturally turn to friends for the real deal on everything from the latest movie to the new cell phones or the hot new restaurant in town.

One great *digital* possibility for promoting buzz is Internet blogs. Right now, our company is working with a major religious organization, and we're encouraging all their supporters who happen to blog to write about the ministry. Considering the size of the organization, we're confident that a serious number of their supporters blog, which should spark a significant online conversation, flooding the Net with positive stories about the ministry.

In the middle of your excitement about national advertising and promotions, never forget the simple things, like taking your message directly to the people who can help you the most.

CHAPTER SEVEN

GREAT DESIGN:
The Language of a Generation

Aesthetics, or styling, has become an accepted unique selling point—on a global basis. In a crowded marketplace, aesthetics is often the only way to make a product stand out.
VIRGINIA POSTRAL, *THE SUBSTANCE OF STYLE*[1]

Governments, dictators, business leaders and global influencers of all kinds have spent centuries trying to discover how to bring together organizations, communities and nations. Time and time again, they've found one answer.

Design.

Early in the life of the Church, the Christian community discovered the transforming power of images. From Byzantine paintings and mosaics to the great art of the Middle Ages and Renaissance and the icons of Eastern Orthodoxy, the Church presented its message through the narrative storytelling of images. Under Communism, Lenin exploited the influence of propaganda posters, and it didn't take long for the kings of American business to investigate the visual power of advertising. For good or bad, since the earliest days of recorded history, the power of design has influenced millions.

And now, once again, design has united a generation.

From the intense graphic design of video games to the pioneering special effects of major motion pictures, from the storyboards of music videos and commercials to high-definition television, young people today speak the language of design. My daughters could retouch digital photos while in elementary school, and by middle school they were accomplished Web designers.

We live in a design-driven generation, and if the Church is going to make an impact, design is the language we must learn.

In Western culture, content has always been king. From the early days of the Hebrew Scriptures, to the spread of Christianity across Western Europe and eventually America, we've been a word-based people. William Tyndale's translation of the Bible into English sparked a revolution of literacy in the sixteenth century; and the greatest missionary efforts of the last few centuries have been the goals of translating and distributing the biblical text to every culture and people group on the planet.

Kathleen and I have begun collecting rare English Bibles. Our collection is very modest, but it's an amazing thing to hold a Bible in your hand that was printed before the first settlers stepped off the ship onto North American soil. Seeing the extreme care that went into the earliest English Bibles has made me realize just how much people of the time valued the written word.

As a result—and rightly so—content has been far more important than form in our art, our writing, our media, our music and our architecture. But today, we live in a design culture, and form has become a critical key to connecting with the public. So while biblical literacy can never be taken for granted, we now face a new challenge: presenting a message of hope to a generation that's more visually sophisticated than any generation in history.

I call design the language of this generation, and although many have criticized the transition of the faith from a text-based culture, we have to realize the change that is happening right now and respond with vigor. In a typical church or nonprofit setting, here are some simple places where strong design can make a difference:

- Print advertising
- Logo design
- Product packaging for books and tape sets
- Business cards and stationery
- Electronic or printed church or ministry newsletters
- Websites
- Email "blasts" to members, partners and supporters
- Event flyers and invitations
- Packaging
- Press releases and electronic press kits
- Posters
- Church program brochures
- Thank-you notes
- Church or ministry facility signage
- Banners
- Television and video programming
- Image magnification
- Church video announcements

There are many more options, but that should give you an idea why talented graphic artists are one of the most coveted employees churches and ministries can find.

Another alternative is finding a graphic design company on the outside and using them for the major projects or to help you design a production style guide to show your in-house graphics team how to use the logo and branding most effectively and appropriately.

> *Beginning today . . . symbols will be replacing words.*
>
> **JODI BERNSTEIN, DIRECTOR, FTC BUREAU OF CONSUMER PROTECTION**

In the secular world, major companies are very strict about using their logo designs. Early in my career, I was asked to write and produce a video presentation for a major oil company in the wake of a disastrous explosion at one of their refineries, causing multiple deaths and hundreds of millions of dollars in damage. The purpose of the video was to document the rebuilding of the refinery and to show their sensitivity to the environment and to families of the deceased.

During the editing phase of the project, I was presented with a 40-page "style guide" that indicated in very precise terms the exact usage of the company's logo and color scheme. In addition, they dispatched a company attorney to sit in the editing suite to verify that I was using the logo correctly. That was a company that realized the power of their corporate brand and wanted to make sure their identity was very carefully presented to the public.

In the book *Branding for Non-Profits: Developing Identity with Integrity*, D. K. Holland asks these key questions during the design phase of a branding project:

- How valid is the concept for the organization?
- How powerful is the concept? Will our primary audiences connect to it on an emotional level?
- How original is the concept? Can we "own" this concept or is it too generic?
- Is the concept clear and focused or is it ambiguous? Can it be interpreted in more ways than one? If so, does it support our cause or undermine it?
- Is the concept versatile or rigid? Does it have legs—in other words, is it flexible enough to be used in a variety of ways that build a brand with depth?
- Can the logo be reduced or enlarged and still maintain its integrity? Can it be used in black and white and remain legible?[2]

A Logo Isn't a Brand

It's important to remember that a logo is not a brand; it's the visual expression of the brand and reflects the DNA of the brand. Most churches and ministries get hung up on the logo, but I never bring in the graphic artist until we've very carefully created the brand story we want to tell. At that point, the artist can help us design a logo that expresses that story to the public.

The key is to share your brand story with the artist and provide enough information about you and your organization. If you've hired a talented designer, then let him (or her) do his job. Although you should feel free to share any ideas you have, let the designer have the artistic freedom to experiment and try some new approaches.

Some artists like to present you with 10 to 20 or more sketches; others prefer 2 to 3. Some like rough pencil sketches, and others like to only show clients finished work. Whatever style the designer prefers, discuss it beforehand and make sure you both understand the parameters, the budget and the expectations.

To maximize outreach in this visually driven age, we need to embrace the power of design. It's not hard to see, because the evidence for great design is everywhere. Just check out the unique design features of new computers or the interior design of coffee shops. Cell phones, automobiles, software, movies—all are examples of a design-driven culture. Better design isn't just decoration; it's connection. Designer Charles Eames said, "Design is a plan for action."

Sure, sixteenth-century Pope Julius could have had the ceiling of the Vatican's Sistine Chapel painted a nice solid color, but he chose to give Michelangelo a little creative challenge. We Christians should have learned something by that, but today we build churches in metal buildings, design boring websites and create tacky book and audiotape and DVD covers. As a producer and media consultant, I have spent decades encouraging clients to realize the power of design to connect with customers and recognize its influence on getting a message heard. I recommend that churches and ministries reconsider worship graphics and images, product packaging, television programming, websites, publications—anything they create—with a new attitude toward design. Rethinking the design elements of a project isn't just a cosmetic issue; it's a fundamental issue about something that connects with the audience or customer on a very deep and significant level.

Don't toss out your Bibles, commentaries, reference books, charts or tables. The power of text will always be critical in telling the eternal story of our faith experience. But without a visual element to your brand, reaching this generation will prove far more difficult than you could possibly imagine. Creating a ministry outreach that presents the gospel in a compelling way that will capture the hearts and minds of the mainstream audience is difficult enough, but a sure ticket into the mindshare of young people is the power of graphic design and visuals.

Great design inspires passion.

Brand Unity

The need for good design happens on a number of levels. First, you establish a strong and evocative logo, which then dictates the visual style of your print look and feel. Second, a style guide is created, usually by your designer, which details how the new logo, color scheme and style should be used throughout the ministry. This will allow your in-house production artists to understand how to use the new style effectively and not undermine the new visual identity.

Third, it creates brand unity, which is the act of unifying all visual outreaches of the ministry so that no matter how someone comes in contact with the church or ministry, they experience the same look and feel.

There are various ministry touch points where customers, church members or supporters may come in contact with the organization:

- Television
- Website
- Brochures and other printed material
- Email notices and blasts
- Business stationery—cards, letterhead, envelopes
- Banners or posters
- Book covers
- Audio CD, DVD, and other product packaging
- Print advertisements in various magazines and newspapers

One of the greatest challenges I face when working with churches and ministries is that most of the time all these products look different. In some cases, the variations are so great that they each look like they were produced by different organizations.

In a media-driven culture filled with advertising clutter, impressions are critical in getting a message across. I'm so busy during a typical day that when something really important comes up, my assistant will often tell me about it, remind me later, send a follow-up email, put it on my calendar, and then add it to my to-do list. Critical messages need to punch through the clutter of all the other issues fighting for my attention.

Your viewers and supporters are experiencing the same type of clutter, and without multiple impressions telling the same story and message, your communication just won't get through.

Brand unity helps make sure the message hits the target by telling the same brand story throughout any touch point your audience might encounter. The message they receive at church supports the visual message they receive in the mail, view on television or encounter on your website. Instead of different visual messages hitting like scattershot, your audience is on the receiving end of a laser beam, receiving your communication with much greater intensity and power.

I can't stress enough the importance of brand unity because of its ultimate impact on the success and effectiveness of your outreach.

CHAPTER EIGHT

THE DARK SIDE OF BRANDING:
The Digital Revolution, Chasing Relevance and the Marketing Conflict

He who marries the spirit of the age soon becomes a widower. As with great art, faith that lasts is faith that answers to higher standards than today's trends.

DEAN INGE, ST. PAUL'S CATHEDRAL IN LONDON

The entire concept of branding often raises such a red flag for Christian believers that I rarely have a conversation about the subject without a debate (often quite lively) about the negative connotations of branding as well. For a multitude of reasons, branding and its close relative, marketing, have gotten a bad reputation in the church, probably as much for its inept execution than anything else. But there are several strong reasons why I continue to keep the dialogue going about branding's relevance to churches, ministries and other nonprofits.

Like most areas of life, the greatest dangers often come out of the strongest positives; so, like a two-edged sword, we need to closely examine all aspects of branding. Through my own experience, I've discovered that the three most dangerous areas of branding are (1) technology, (2) chasing relevance, and (3) a key conflict with the concept of marketing.

> *It has become appallingly obvious that our technology has exceeded our humanity.*
>
> **ALBERT EINSTEIN**

The Dangers of the Digital Revolution

It would be a profound mistake to realize the possibilities of telling the right brand story about you, your church or your ministry without also understanding that like most media issues, branding can have unintended consequences and sometimes seriously negative implications for the culture. From what I call the "pornografication" of our culture through the sexualizing of nearly everything, to the loss of community, digital technology has implications that we have yet to fully understand.

Mercer Schuchardt captured the concern very well in an online post on theooze.com:

> If sport is the religion of the modern age, then Nike has successfully become the official church. It is a church whose icon serves as an allegory that formulates salvation in a special parabolical and symbolic language. The Swoosh is a window on the border between this world and the other, between your existing self (you overweight slob) and your Nike self (you god of fitness), where salvation is the attainment of the athletic Nietzschean ideal: no fear, no mercy, no second place. The Swoosh is a true religious icon in that it serves as a representation of the reality and as a participant in the reality; you do after all, have to wear something to attain this special salvation, so why not something emblazoned with that Swoosh?

How powerful is the zeal spawned by the cult of Nike? So powerful, that we kill for it. Since 1991, five Americans have been shot to death for the Nikes on their feet. Lt. Thomas Malacek, the officer handling one of the cases, said, "It's becoming a growing problem, because apparently these items have a lot more identity value than in the past."

Well, you say, the kids are crazy these days, and there's a whole slew of other factors involved in each one of these deaths: Poverty. Race. Violence. Family breakdown.

Sure, but it still begs the question: How come no one's ever died for a pair of Reeboks?

Or Adidas?

Or Filas?[1]

As I've mentioned before, some branding critics have pointed to the sweatshops of the Third World, mass producing tennis shoes, the pollution created by factories, or even the globalization of the economy. While those issues are all serious, I don't see them as a result of the rise in global branding and marketing. Certainly sweatshops existed long before American companies starting manufacturing tennis shoes; unsafe factories were killing people in the nineteenth century, and globalization has always been the inevitable result of expanding markets.

Global corporations are in business to make money, and in a secular society, many do whatever it takes. Using branding as well as a multitude of other business and marketing tools, they're going to wreak havoc on local economies, child labor laws, pollution guidelines, and more. But we don't stop using good accounting principles because of the bookkeeping abuses of Enron.

We live in a horribly fallen world, but that doesn't excuse us from making our voice heard in the public square and trying to change the culture. As Christians, we have the highest responsibility toward our fellow man, Christian and non-Christian alike, and should be working to make sure that technology serves the public good.

My personal concerns about the negative implications of digital media and branding revolve around our sense of community and space—how it affects our personal relationships and changes our behavior.

In the first chapter, I mentioned the *Los Angeles Times* newspaper story reporting on cell phone use in Korea that revealed remarkable information about where our digital culture may be heading. They discovered that Korean teenagers make up to 90 cell phone calls a day, and social scientists are now beginning to correlate high cell use with rising rates of depression in that country. Here at home, I've noticed that many young people value their digital life as much (if not more) than their real life. A friend of my daughter sent 2,500 text messages last month from her cell phone (that's more than 84 per day).

The Transparent Generation

Privacy matters very little for a generation that grew up on the Internet. Teenagers post the most intimate details of their lives on the Web, with little thought about how it might affect them later in life. It doesn't take much to find the most compromising information and photos about people, and an alarming number of pedophiles have found their targets simply through browsing public information willingly posted by young people.

Drunken party pictures, details of romances or sexual encounters, even plots to murder friends or relatives have been found on sites created by kids who seemed to be otherwise quite normal. In the digital world, young people don't have the sense of personal privacy that older generations took for granted.

Blunt conversations, personal information, candid revelations—literally everything is being posted by people with little understanding of the consequences. Far too many young people have video cameras connected to their computers and are broadcasting pictures and movies directly from their bedrooms, with little or no control of who might be watching.

As a result, to "Google" someone has become an accepted part of social encounters. A Harris Interactive Poll found that already one of every four business people automatically search the Web for the name of an associate or colleague before meeting them in person.

The question becomes, How does this transparency impact their reception of our media messages? Does that change our strategy? If nothing else, it's certainly a reminder to be very careful what we post for the world to see.

Online Community

At the time of this writing, Facebook (facebook.com) is one of the strongest brands on the Internet. It's so popular that it has become the social hub for millions of people, particularly teenagers. And in case you've been asleep at the wheel, here are a few interesting Facebook statistics, which by the time you read this will no doubt be much higher.

Although MySpace.com is still the largest online social networking portal on the web, Facebook now has more than 55 million active users. Since January 2007, Facebook has experienced an average of 250,000 new members *each day*. The number of active users double every six months. People spend an average of 20 minutes on the site per visit, with the fastest-growing demographic group being those 25 years of age and older. It is also the number one photo sharing site on the web, with more than 14 million photos uploaded daily.

The power of a site that regularly visited by that many people is staggering. Today, major corporations, politicians, advertisers and celebrities create Facebook or Myspace accounts in the hope of reaching a larger audience. On the other side of the coin, these millions of visitors are doing it *alone*. Although the Internet is a communications medium and people use it for email, instant messaging, and other types of communication, it's a solitary physical activity—one person sitting at a single computer.[2]

While the Internet is growing, our real friendships are shrinking.

The Knight-Ridder news service recently released a study indicating that Americans are reporting fewer and fewer close friends.[3] In 1985, pollsters noted that the average person reported having three close friends, but by 2006, it was only two. And the number who say they have no one to discuss important matters with has doubled to one in four.[4] The social implications are significant—from no friends to visit people in the hospital and weakened bonds during crisis to fewer watchdogs to deter neighborhood crime, and a lack of community.

From a church and ministry perspective, this trend has significant implications. As Shane Hipps relates in his book *The Hidden Power of Electronic Culture*:

> Churches have begun to use blogs, chat areas, and electronic bulletin boards in their efforts to build community. Yet there remains the danger of people finding connection through these electronic forms and believing they have found genuine intimacy. This can cause them to miss out on authentic community with the people they worship with each week.[5]

As I write this, *USA Today* published a story called "Meet my 5,000 new best pals." It's about the phenomenon of

MySpace.com and the growth of online "friends" that use that site as a community. Although the teenager featured in the story lists 5,036 friends on her site, she admits that she has virtually no relationship with at least 90 percent of those people. Today, "friending," as they call it, has become a status symbol, with many young people afraid to start college without hundreds of online "friends" to give them some sort of perceived validity.[6]

Friendships without relationship—it's new territory for most of us.

I was struck recently when my assistant traveled to South Carolina to attend her grandmother's funeral. Even though I grew up in nearby North Carolina, it was a welcome reminder of the sense of community a small town engenders. After the funeral service itself, my assistant was astonished at the number of church members, former coworkers and friends who came to the family home with fried chicken, casseroles, vegetables, cake, pies and other food for the family. They turned out in huge numbers to simply sit with the family and comfort them.

When you die, how many of your MySpace friends will come to comfort your family? How many Internet chat room members will show up at the funeral?

Think about it. When was the last time you actually visited your neighbors? Activities that we took for granted as children, such as interacting with the family next door, happens rarely if ever. Fewer people have lifelong relationships from church, and activities that friends used to help us with—moving, painting or fixing the car—we've now farmed out to professionals.

Technology, branding and marketing has brought wonderful changes into our lives. Computers, cell phones, personal digital assistants (PDA), and more, aid our personal lives, businesses, and humanitarian and evangelistic work. The media alerts us to local and national emergencies, keeps us updated on important (and sometimes not so important) news and gives us a tool for sharing our faith on a global scale. But at the same time, we need to be aware of how the digital universe is impacting our relationships. Thanks to the news media, we're already aware of online predators who directly target minors for sex, Internet scams that prey on seniors, and the explosion of online pornography.

One of my biggest concerns is how technology affects our behavior.

Addicted to Electronic Connection

I used to enjoy the radio or CD player when driving, but now I feel compelled to do business on my cell phone. I can't seem to sit in a car by myself without "doing something." At the same time, I've become a Zen master at email. I can download it through wired or wireless connections, my cell card or through our server from any other computer on the planet. But I try to control that impulse now.

While filming a project in London last year, I had an experience that shocked me into realizing how much I needed boundaries around my email habits. Kathleen and I had finished breakfast and were waiting in the lobby for the film crew to bring our vehicles around to the front of the hotel. While waiting, I decided to visit the restroom, where I encountered a professional-looking businessman.

I noticed that at the same time he was using the restroom, he was also checking his email on his handheld device.

I couldn't help myself, so I leaned over and said, "Brother, that's bondage."

He replied in a perfect British accent, "Sir, you have no idea how serious this bondage is."

I walked out of that restroom, pulled my handheld PDA out of my pocket, gave it to Kathleen and haven't touched it since. I decided that I never want to get to the place where I feel such a compulsion to answer my email.

Technology is moving forward, so does that mean we are destined to live our lives in isolation? Although the situation is certainly getting worse, there are a few things we can do to get our lives back: (1) *Take a break from media,* (2) *develop personal relationships, and* (3) *encourage closer community in our churches.*

1. Take a Break from Media

I love movies, television and the Internet, but from time to time it's important to take a break from them. When you get that urge to check your email during the pastor's message, or text message the person in the next cubicle at work, it might be time for a media fast. Take a day or two off and see what happens. Recently, an email glitch deleted about 30 messages in my inbox. I was horrified, but guess what? Nothing happened. I didn't lose any clients, no projects missed a deadline and no one else even noticed. Learn to turn it off!

You have to master the tool, or believe me, it will master you.

I've also discovered the importance of using email for non-emergency issues only. If you need an answer right away, use the phone. I've started to train my employees, clients and other relationships that sometimes I answer email quickly, and sometimes I don't. This helps you overcome the feeling that there's an email out there you absolutely have to answer *right now*. Rest easy, because if it's important, they'll call.

2. Be More Aggressive about Developing Personal Relationships

In a world in which few people have close friends, expand your community and get to know people. Enlarge your network of really close friends. Perhaps it's because I was raised before the digital age that I still value face-to-face communication far more than phone conversations or email. But I'm not so sure about my daughter's generation. We have two wonderful daughters, and pretty much the only area in which we have real disagreements is the cell phone bill. They're always pushing for more minutes, because their cell phones have become an indispensable part of their lives. I'm speaking at conferences across the country, and I'm involved in running two media companies producing projects literally around the world. But my daughters use their cell phones more than I do.

Earlier, I encouraged you to save all your "emergency" issues for the phone rather than email. But even with that advice, there are certain conversations I believe you should have face to face. If you have a serious disagreement with someone, need to fire an employee or deliver other grave news, email or phone isn't the answer unless it's the only method available. For serious heart-to-heart conversations, conduct them in person. Email almost completely lacks nuance, and with phones, you can't read facial expressions or adequately convey emotions.

On that issue, never *ever* criticize someone personally through an email. I've learned this the hard way. Once you hit the "send" button, you have lost control of that note, and you have no idea who will read it or how it might be used. The recipient may be your friend right now, but if the tables are turned, he or she could easily use that email against you later. If you need to reprimand or criticize in any way, do it directly to the person. And most important, if you need to talk about a third person in a negative light, do that in person as well. More people than you would imagine are humiliated, fired, misunderstood or have their careers and futures ruined because of this issue.

3. Encourage Closer Community in Your Church

The church is the original community. The Bible spends a great deal of time talking about the fellowship of believers. Consider creating more face-to-face activities that encourage friendships and develop deeper relationships among church members. Just as my assistant discovered at her grandmother's funeral, churches that truly believe in community make a dramatic difference in the lives of their members.

The explosion of cell groups is an indicator of the strength of community building. Today's mega-churches aren't a single group of 2,000 people. They're a hundred groups of 20 people each. Those individuals and families are the core relationships that members create, and if they're developed correctly, they become the thread that makes the church happen.

Technology is critical to our lives, but where are we going as a culture if our digital life replaces our real life? The lure of technology means that we must be active in developing personal relationships. Remember, mass media is a wonderful tool, but ultimately, real community happens face to face.

> *I believe I am not mistaken when I say that Christianity is a demanding and serious religion. When it is delivered as easy and amusing, it is another kind of religion altogether.*
>
> **NEIL POSTMAN, MEDIA CRITIC**

The Trivial Culture

Another great concern about a media-driven culture is television's tendency to trivialize everything it touches. In an earlier age, pastors and ministry leaders were brilliant thinkers and intellectuals. Men like Jonathan Edwards, George Whitefield and Charles Finney were all highly educated and had exceptional speaking and writing skills. It was typical of their time to speak for more than two hours, and during pubic debates, each side would speak for at least an hour, back and forth, so that the entire event unfolded over a five- to six-hour period.

I grew up in the South attending evangelistic "camp meetings" with my grandmother. Many of these meetings were virtual festivals, with picnics, activities for the kids, potluck dinners on the ground, and even overnight housing; and very often, the preaching would last all day and far into the evening. One of my earliest memories is of sitting on a handmade quilt on a sawdust floor, listening to preachers pound the pulpit long past my bedtime.

Compare that time frame to the length of programming for typical television preachers today. With most programs running 30 minutes, by the time we edit the opening, closing, a couple of special video segments or product offers and perhaps an interview, the preaching segment gets little more than 12 to 16 minutes on most programs. That time constraint has also trickled into many Sunday services as well. I visited a church just a few weeks ago in which the pastor preaches no more than 12 to 15 minutes on a Sunday. He feels that in a highly distracted culture, 15 minutes is about all he can demand of his audience.

Much of what we call worship has become show business, as pastors feel the need to entertain congregations in order to justify their time. As a media producer (and an easily distracted person myself), I'm the first to protest a boring service or anything that doesn't keep the momentum moving forward. I'm told that a journalist once asked suspense movie director Alfred Hitchcock about the perfect length for a movie. His reply was, "As long as their butt can hold out."

I tend to feel the same way about church services.

But at the same time, I wonder how the compulsion to entertain has damaged the sacred experience. After all, there is something to the mystery of our faith, and when Christianity is adapted to an entertainment medium, how much of the serious pursuit of the divine has been sacrificed? It's difficult to portray the transcendent through the same medium that broadcasts the World Wrestling Federation or *American Idol.* The result is the frustrating sight of our faith fraying around the edges.

Sadly, it's not about raising the congregation to a higher level; it's about bringing the ministry down to theirs.

One pastor dresses like Elvis every Sunday to draw more interest. Many churches mix movie clips with sermons, rock 'n' roll with worship, and sports metaphors with the services, most of which I often support.

Creativity is important, but at what expense?

In our well-intentioned efforts to reach the largest audience possible, we've forgotten that the Christian faith isn't always easy, and this generation is starting to recognize the disconnect.

One 30-year-old national magazine editor sent me an email recently that summed up the entire point. We'd been discussing the question of what's wrong with Christian television, and his response was a wake-up call: "Who cares? Anyone my age, who's grown up on television, knows you can't take anything you see on it seriously, whether it's religion or not. It's all trivial and ultimately doesn't matter. Television is an entertainment medium, so why would I ever watch a Christian program on TV?"

Television has trivialized news, educational programming and politics. And now it has done the same to religion.

In his book *Amusing Ourselves to Death*, media critic and theorist Neil Postman describes the competing visions of the future of technology outlined by George Orwell in his book *1984*, and by Aldous Huxley in *Brave New World*:

> What Orwell feared were those who would ban books. What Huxley feared was that there would be no reason to ban a book, for there would be no one who wanted to read one. Orwell feared those who would deprive us of information. Huxley feared those who would give us so much that we would be reduced to passivity and egoism. Orwell feared the truth would be concealed from us. Huxley feared the truth would be drowned in a sea of irrelevance. Orwell feared that we would become a captive culture. Huxley feared that we would become a trivial culture, preoccupied with some equivalent of the feelies, the orgy porgy, and the centrifugal bumblepuppy. As Huxley remarked in *Brave New World Revisited*, the civil libertarians and rationalists who are ever on the alert to oppose tyranny "failed to take into account man's almost infinite appetite for distractions." In short, Orwell feared that what we hate will ruin us. Huxley feared that what we love will ruin us.[7]

There is no question that Huxley was the prophetic voice. Thanks to television, we're consumed by the trivial. Thanks to the Internet, we are drowning in a sea of information and yet unable to truly communicate. And thanks to email, we live our lives under the compulsion that there's an important message out there worth interrupting everything else to read.

A wealth of information creates a poverty of attention.

HERBERT SIMON

Americans are drowning in information and starving for attention.

PASTOR RICK WARREN

In a digital age, authenticity may be the ultimate scorecard for success. But it's not the traditional definition of authenticity we're talking about here. In the past, authenticity had to do with *proof*. A famous painting was authentic because it could be proven beyond a shadow of a doubt that it was real. A prized autograph was authentic because there was documentation to back up the claim. Authenticity used to be about truth, but today it's about preference.

Today, authenticity has to do with *feeling*. When someone likes you or your ministry, they feel like you're "authentic." It has nothing to do with a qualitative decision, research or what is true; it's simply an emotional response. Be very careful when people describe you or your ministry as authentic, because in a postmodern value system, it's only meaning is that you resonate with that particular person.

It may be your clothing, mannerisms, age, personal style or type of program, but whatever it is, it probably has little to do with your ministry's real value or credibility. However, we still need to recognize the issue and respond.

Breaking the Spell of Trivialization

So how do we break the spell of trivialization? Do we take the Luddite path to oblivion or make a real attempt to wrestle the monster to the ground? I honestly don't hold much hope that the majority of Christian media will get much better. As a result, I believe there are two key strategies we must begin as soon as possible.

Key Strategy #1: Find Innovative Christian Communicators

First, we must find the innovative Christian communicators who really want to make a difference. While there will always be a place in the media for important and timely preaching, that source of programming will not be the driver of Christian media as it has been in the past. Today there are independent producers creating low-budget movies, short films, Internet radio programming, innovative websites, podcasts, and more, and we must find them and encourage what they're doing.

That's not meant to discourage pastors or ministry leaders from creating compelling programming based on teaching and preaching. Many of our clients are preaching ministries, and we've helped them create brand identities that capture significant audiences. But at the same time, look for a wider range of programming options and the creative men and women who can make them happen.

The first generation of religious media communicators were for the most part pastors and evangelists who seized upon radio and eventually television as a way to extend their ministries. Their strength was the power of the message. They preached with passion and excitement and were relentless in their mission to spread the gospel.

But their weakness was packaging—the various elements such as lighting, set design, wardrobe, directing and editing that make up a quality program. They were preachers after all and had little idea of creativity, production techniques, contemporary graphics, branding or compelling visuals. Their resulting programs shared an important message but were often corny, low quality and poorly produced. To nonbelievers, they appeared fake, cheesy and insincere.

Today the driving force behind Christian media is emerging from behind the camera. Younger filmmakers and producers want to expand the horizon of religious media, try new techniques and create projects for wide-ranging audiences. These producers are looking beyond telethons to fund their projects and are experimenting with commercial sponsorship, grants, product placement, and more.

And now, preachers are catching the vision as well. Just because you preach doesn't mean the program has to be old-fashioned; and through innovative production techniques, a younger generation of pastors and ministry leaders are discovering how to reach an audience and create a response.

Key Strategy #2: Expand the Conversation

Second, we need to continue this conversation and expand it through our personal networks. Once we understand the trivializing nature of television, for instance, it loses its power over us. If we can teach men, women and families how to consume media correctly, we can make huge strides in using media more effectively. I always encourage pastors to have "movie nights" at church to view current films and engage the audience in a discussion. The media is the single greatest influence over the members of your congregation, and yet few pastors teach about its impact and effects.

We've allowed an entire generation to grow up helpless in the face of a force that literally consumes their lives. Teach about it, discuss it and keep this conversation going. As innovative writer and pastor Erwin McManus said recently to an audience at the

National Religious Broadcasters conference:

> God is already having a conversation with the culture, and our job is to intersect that conversation where *they* are, not where *we* are. We've got to move away from creating programming that is comfortable for us, into programming that engages the audience where they are at the moment.[8]

I was raised in a church that felt it wasn't strictly a sin to go to a movie, but if Jesus returned while you were inside the theater, all bets were off. Fortunately, today more and more pastors are embracing the media and aren't afraid to use it as a teaching tool or point of discussion. Most people simply use the media because it's there, not because they understand its hold over them. And if we can train people to encounter TV, radio, the Internet and other media with discernment and skill, we can turn the tables and break the spell.

> *Never have Christians pursued relevance more strenuously; never have Christians been more irrelevant.*
>
> **OS GUINNESS**

The Danger of Chasing Relevance

Ask a typical pastor or ministry leader what they want to accomplish with their ministry, programs or products, and chances are, you'll hear the words "be relevant." "Relevance" has become the hot buzzword today—especially in the Christian media world—and applies to church services, TV and radio programming, books, music, and outreaches of all kinds. In this culture, everyone wants to be relevant.

I've spent my career helping the Church speak the language of the culture, and being contemporary and relevant is part of that equation. But in that process, I've discovered that most people work so hard to be relevant that they spin hopelessly into irrelevance.

How? Most pastors and Christian leaders mistake relevant for trendy. They hope that if they wear the right clothes, use the right words, get just the right haircut, speak on current topics, or play the right music, they'll somehow be perceived as relevant.

Robyn Waters has written the insightful book *The Trendmaster's Guide: Get a Jump on What Your Customer Wants Next.* It has become a popular guide for business and marketing directors trying to create the next hot product based on current trends. I bought the book expecting to find out just how silly and shallow American business has become, but as I read, I realized that the writer was on to something that most pastors and Christian leaders have missed about tracking trends:

> Trends are indicators that point to what's going on in the hearts and minds of consumers. And there's a big difference between a trend tracker and a Trendmaster. A trend tracker looks at the signs to help his or her business stay up to the minute. A Trendmaster, however, uses the trend information to determine where that minute is going. Trendmasters start out by observing a trend, but then they translate that trend information into a direction that makes sense for their companies and their customers.[9]

Jesus was upset at the religious leaders of His day because they knew how to interpret the appearance of the sky, but they didn't understand the signs of the times.

It's not about chasing the latest new thing. It's about interpreting what that new thing means to your audience.

I recently spoke at a major media conference with another lecturer who considered himself a futurist. He was a college professor and had written numerous books on the future of entertainment and media. He spoke for nearly an hour, sharing interesting statistics he had no doubt gathered from industry research and journals. It was interesting stuff, but nothing the audience couldn't have found for themselves. After he spoke, we participated on a panel discussion, and I asked him about his recommendations for communicators in light of the statistics and data he had shared. His response surprised me, and the audience as well:

"That's your problem."

He had billed himself as a futurist but had done little more than compile data on technology from available books and other sources. When it came to *application*—how to apply that data to the issues we face in media today—he was a blank. Like the religious leaders of Jesus' day, he could see the appearance of the sky but couldn't interpret the signs of the times.

Being relevant is something far bigger and more significant than constantly trying to figure out what's *next.*

Robyn Waters goes on to say, "It's easy to get caught up in the frenzy of tracking trends and to forget about the really good things that seem to last forever. Don't be so focused on the next big thing that you forget about those things that are always in style."[10]

Her book isn't religious at all; it's designed for business. But it's not bad advice for pastors and Christian leaders: Relevance isn't about chasing trends; it's about standing the test of time.

The French philosopher and culture critic Simone Weil said, "To be always relevant, you have to say things which are eternal." Ultimate relevance is about the principles that last—eternal truths with a capital *T*.

That's no excuse to wear tasteless clothes, sport bad haircuts, have a choir with no talent or use out-of-date techniques. (I'd personally feel I had done my job on the earth if we could rid Christian TV of fireplaces, plants, blue curtains, bad hair and tacky furniture.) To speak in the living room of the society, you must first get in the door. In Acts 17, the apostle Paul gave us the perfect example of how to engage the culture, and it still resonates today, especially when it comes to the media: No matter how brilliant your message, it doesn't matter if no one listens.

But when they do listen, make sure you're not trying to chase relevance.

In that vain search, we've exchanged powerful preaching for positive thinking; we've exchanged classic Christian doctrines for "what's practical"; and we've exchanged our unique calling to become simply another lifestyle choice.

This isn't new. As early as 1966, the World Council of Churches created the strange mandate, "The world must set the agenda for the church."

The compromise in pursuit of relevance has damaged both sides of the political spectrum. Liberal churches have gone to bed with the cultural and philosophical assumptions of their time, desperately trying to legitimize themselves with the culture. The church has allowed science to direct its focus, politics to chart its direction and cultural accommodation to set its vision for the future.

But the more conservative evangelical church has done as much damage pursuing the business and marketing mindset. Without a clear vision of our unique character and purpose before the world, we've uncritically adopted business principles, marketing savvy and pop culture. Os Guinness wrote, "A great part of the evangelical community has made an historic shift. It has transferred authority from *Sola Scriptura* (by Scripture alone) to *Sola Cultura* (by culture alone)."[11]

We've already seen the damage of this cultural accommodation, from the dramatic rise in pornography among pastors, a focus on finances and prosperity preaching, and a lack of passion for classic Christian outreaches like global missions. Today we have pastors who experience ugly divorces but never leave the pulpits, rampant nepotism within ministry families, and alcoholism among ministry leaders, but no one courageous enough to report it.

From the legacy of a world in which Martin Luther stood up to the secular powers and said, "Here I stand, so help me God, I can do no other," or William Tyndale, who defied the British crown and was strangled and burned at the stake for giving us the remarkable gift of the Bible in English, today we have turned from God's authority to the authority of the culture.

In our well-intentioned efforts to draw large audiences, expand our congregations and increase our impact in the world, we've lost our unique character before the world to the point where the culture sees little difference between becoming a Christian and becoming a Lakers fan.

As Philip Denneson and James Street wrote in their book *Selling Out the Church*, "The marketing mentality readily assumes that the church of Jesus Christ is fundamentally like other organizations and businesses."[12]

Chasing relevance is a hopeless proposition, because what's relevant changes as styles, trends and seasons change. What was wonderfully relevant last year might simply get a laugh now.

Instead, we must build our lives and ministries around the eternal verities—the things that last, that are eternal.

Pastors, ministry leaders and conference hosts have followed hot on the trail of motivation, self-esteem, prosperity, faith teaching, positive thinking—all of which have certainly been high on the relevance meter in their time. But while we were trying so hard to be relevant, guess what? An apparent nonbeliever—Dan Brown—wrote a ludicrous novel called *The Da Vinci Code* about the supposed origins of Christianity that as of this writing millions of people are reading and millions more are watching as a movie. Sure the novel is "historical hooey," as movie star Tom Hanks has said, but the book's success tells me that millions of people are asking serious questions about the beginnings of the Christian faith, the divinity of Jesus and the validity of believing in God. While the Church was chasing relevance, a nonbeliever realized the aching hunger for people to learn about the deeper things of God.

It doesn't matter if you're a pastor, ministry leader or simply a church member sharing your faith with a friend or coworker. If you want to be remembered and have your message mean as much to someone 100 years from now as it does at this moment, then reach for a higher goal.

Ultimately, to truly be relevant, stop trying so hard to be relevant.

> *Church marketers overlook that Jesus, in being faithful to his calling, also drove people away. Some of Jesus' most radical and disturbing teachings were given at junctures when crowds were the largest.*
>
> **PHILIP KENNESON AND JAMES STREET**

The Marketing Conflict

The online dictionary.com defines "marketing" as:

> The act of buying or selling in a market, and the total of activities involved in the transfer of goods from the producer or seller to the consumer or buyer, including advertising, shipping, storing, and selling. The origin of the term is from 1555–65.[13]

Another online source, investopedia.com, gives a more focused definition for our purposes:

> The activities of a company associated with buying and selling a product or service. It includes advertising, selling and delivering products to people. People who work in marketing departments of companies try to get the attention of target audiences by using slogans, packaging design, celebrity endorsements and general media exposure. The four "Ps" of marketing are product, place, price and promotion.[14]

Investopedia.com goes on to say:

> Many people believe that marketing is just about advertising or sales. However, marketing is everything a company does to acquire customers and maintain a

> relationship with them. Even the small tasks like writing thank-you letters, playing golf with a prospective client, returning calls promptly and meeting with a past client for coffee can be thought of as marketing. The ultimate goal of marketing is to match a company's products and services to the people who need and want them, and thereby ensure profitability.[15]

When I studied for my master's degree in journalism, I spent a great deal of time with fear and trembling on the subject of marketing and have since spent years in the field working with churches, ministry and secular clients. From my earliest exposure to marketing, sitting in a University of Oklahoma classroom, I discovered that marketing is far more than just advertising and selling a product. It's a very complex discipline involving pricing formulas, financial markets, packaging research, strategy, demographics and the business/customer exchange.

In fact, in 1985, the American Marketing Association articulated it this way:

> Marketing is the process of planning and executing the conception, pricing, promotion, and distribution of ideas, goods and services to create exchanges that will satisfy individual and organizational objectives.[16]

I focus on this issue because in the vast majority of religious organizations (as in the vast majority of companies), few people really understand the concept of marketing. I've sat in meetings where someone was assigned the position of marketing director simply because that person had experience in sales. Or a graphic designer became marketing director because people assumed she understood advertising. Or in the worst cases, the company president or business leader has a son or daughter who seems to be "creative," so they get assigned to the marketing department.

Most church and ministry marketing efforts are not only inept, but they're also catastrophic. In fact, I would put forth that marketing may be one of the most misused techniques and disciplines in the church today.

Is marketing important?

Absolutely.

Then why do we screw it up?

I would suggest a new definition of marketing when it comes to the work of the church:

When I view my role as a branding or media consultant, I view that role as simply placing the church or ministry in the best possible light.

It's that simple.

My job is to put as many people as possible in front of that pastor, evangelist, television program, movie or event. Then, I expect that pastor to preach a message without compromise and with the power that comes from the anointing of the Holy Spirit. My goal is for people to have a life-changing encounter with God. But if the message drives them away—as Jesus' often did—that's fine too.

In a less than formal expression, my job is to put butts in the seats.

For too many years, the church has tried to pre-qualify its audience. We only wanted people who were cleaned up and well mannered. We wanted people who dressed up for services. We wanted people of a certain income or race. Worse, we tried lame promotional gimmicks to generate a crowd. Growing up in the South of the fifties and sixties, I watched pastors sit on flagpoles, shave their heads, get dropped in dunking tanks filled with water, survive eating contests, and more, which I attest attracted a pretty weird group.

These were well-meaning people with the best of intentions. I've discovered that when it comes to marketing a church, even the worst offenders are motivated by the right purpose: the goal of reaching out to the largest audience possible. As a result, while I like to enjoy poking fun at some of the Christian stunts and "Jesus Junk" out there, I'm not a cynic. I don't take the path of those who ridicule, humiliate or criticize people as if they were purposely trying to damage the character and reputation of the church (although that's exactly what sometimes happens).

In 2006, a respected Australian broadcaster named Andrew Denton produced a documentary film on the National Religious Broadcasters. Originally, his intention was to document how faith informed President George Bush's politics, but on a stop at the national convention of Christian broadcasters, he was mesmerized. He interviewed numerous personalities in the industry (including me) over the five-day period that the convention took place, but the most interesting scenes were filmed simply walking up and down the aisles of the exhibit halls at the event as he talked to people at random.

He interviewed people selling TV time, marketing new and unique Bibles, bronze sculptures, health food, religious trinkets, trips to Israel, and much more. Many of the booths had nothing overtly to do with broadcasting, but they were more than eager to be interviewed on television.

There were a lot of odd folks in the mix, and Andrew brilliantly just let them talk. He didn't condemn or embarrass, but simply let them tell their story, and by doing so, they often made themselves look strange and out of touch with the culture.

It was a perfect example of some people who have been communicating the same way for decades, and while the culture has changed, they've held the course. Now they seem outdated, out of touch and quaint. They are the leftovers of the early days of the industry, the ones who are supposed to be professional Christian communicators but have little connection to a mainstream audience today.

By the time Andrew interviewed me, he was fascinated with religious broadcasters, and we had a lively discussion of the strengths and weakness of using the media to impact the culture with a religious message.

The resulting film was called *God on My Side* and debuted at a highly regarded film festival in Sydney, Australia, followed up by a theatrical movie release across the country, and eventually a prime-time broadcast on a major Australian TV network.

I was speaking at a media conference in Australia a year or so later, and my wife and I sat down with Andrew at a coffee shop across the street from his office to discuss the movie and to catch up. He said that after the broadcast of his documentary, he was disconcerted at some friends who told him, "Good job, Andrew. Way to stick it to those con-artists in religious media." Others were thrilled that he had somehow exposed the charlatans in the Christian broadcasting world.

Andrew told them they had missed the point. He said that the one thing he walked away with from the religious broadcasting conference was that above all, these were absolutely sincere people. They honestly believed in what they were doing and were committed to what they believed was right—so much so that it was actually surprising and moving to him as well.

And yet, the overall response to the film was how inept, crooked and out of touch Christian broadcasters seem to the world. The vast majority of the film was simply letting the people talk and tell their stories.

Much of the Church is plagued by well-meaning individuals who damage our credibility and witness because they express their faith in a way that seems so out of touch and odd.

Good People, Bad Ideas

What we need to realize is the fundamental point of being in the world but not of the world. This is a very real tension between wanting to attract the largest possible audience while knowing that our very message will drive many away.

When I work with secular companies, our marketing goal is to remove anything that would hinder the full acceptance of the product. We want potential customers to fall in love with our athletic shoes, coffee, furniture or candy. We want to fix anything that could possibly be a reason they might hesitate to purchase the product.

But with the Christian faith, our goal is a bit different. We want as many people as possible to have the opportunity to hear the gospel, but we also know that we can't compromise, water down or modify the product. Maintaining the integrity of the Christian message is without discussion or debate. Therefore, we aim high, knowing that some seed will fall on rocky places. Not everyone will get through the narrow way (see Matt. 7:14).

In Acts 2, it is recorded that about 3,000 people were added to the Church in one day. That's a marketer's dream. After all, living things grow. The Church should be growing and its outreaches expanding. I believe very strongly in the marketing principles of getting the message out, sharing it in the best possible way and then believing God for the harvest.

That last element—believing God for the harvest—might be another very misunderstood element of church and ministry marketing. I can't guarantee success to my clients. In fact, it's not my job. God gives the increase. We can plan, create brilliant advertising materials, promote the event in the best possible light and attract thousands. But once the message is preached or shared, the convicting power of the Holy Spirit takes over. In that sense, it's not my job to win the lost; it's God's.

Many people rightly criticize church and ministry marketing because they've seen it done so poorly, have inaccurate expectations of the results or rightly worry about its excesses. I've discovered two key things to consider in effective marketing: First, don't change who you are. Second, stop trying to make the church identical to every other organization in the culture.

Don't Change Who You Are

You are who you are. God has called you to be unique and different. The world isn't looking for another Joel Osteen, Joyce Meyer, Charles Stanley, Beth Moore, Billy Graham, Tony Evans, Ed Young or T. D. Jakes. They just might be looking for *you*. If an advertising or marketing consultant tries to change your unique style, gifts or calling, then you're on the wrong track from the beginning. A great marketer will take the time to understand who you are, what your personal and ministry gifts are, what your vision for ministry really is, and focus on that. It's not about *changing* your calling; it's about *celebrating* your calling.

Should you change that dumpy suit, a bad accent or the lime-green carpet in the church? Probably. Don't let a bad package pre-qualify your audience. Remove any boundaries that would keep people from hearing your message, but in the process, don't lose the message itself.

Stop Trying to Make Your Church Identical to Others

In our well-intentioned effort to make the secular culture comfortable with the Christian message, we often take away the very things that make us distinctive. People don't worry that screaming fans will turn off potential ticket buyers for football games, that traditional customs at Jewish weddings will drive friends away, or that weird initiation rites will stop college students from joining fraternities and sororities.

And yet today we're terrified that raising our hands in church will hurt attendance, that prayer for the sick will make us seem cultic, or that baptism during the Sunday service would seem out of place.

At a national media conference sponsored by a major religious denomination, I had the opportunity to meet with the head of communication for the entire organization. I asked him about the biggest challenge the denomination was facing.

He replied, "Oh, that's simple. It's drums."

"Drums?"

"That's right. We may even have a national schism over the use of drums in the church. It's a huge battle right now, and it's literally tearing some churches apart."

I sat there in shock for a minute, and then said, "I thought that was a bridge we crossed in the sixties and seventies in most churches."

"Not in ours," he said.

We major in the minors while the real distinctiveness of our faith is lost to the world.

Certainly negative issues like doctrinal errors, a poorly prepared sermon or a church with no vision should be examined, but in the process, we can't lose the positive distinctives that have made the Christian Church a force that transformed Western civilization.

Phil Pringle pastors Christian City Church in Oxford Falls, Australia, a suburb of Sydney. I recently visited the church and spent some time talking about his love of the media, and how it has impacted the church. Phil has been frustrated by the limitations of traditional Christian radio and television, so he's exploring Youtube.com and posts short videos on a regular basis. I asked him about his branding, and he said something very interesting. His family comes from the Pentecostal tradition, and early in his ministry he saw many other growing churches pulling away from their Pentecostal and Charismatic roots. In an effort to reach the widest possible audience, they were changing their worship and preaching style to something more middle of the road.

Seeing that change happening to so many churches, Phil did just the opposite. He realized that his distinctive was his Pentecostal tradition, so rather than back away like so many others were doing, he focused on the gifts of the Spirit. As a result, his church has exploded, and a new generation of young people looking for a profound Charismatic and Pentecostal experience is flocking to the church.

Phil Pringle understands the power of being distinctive in ministry.

Effective marketing doesn't mean making the church appear like a stockholder's meeting at IBM.

Perhaps we've had to rely on marketing simply because nothing else is happening inside the church itself. The great tragedy today is how anemic so many churches have become. Three thousand people were added to the Early Church in one day because Peter preached a message of power and authority.

The Bible reports that the audience was "cut to the heart" and immediately asked "What shall we do?" (see Acts 2:37).

Now that's action! That's direct response. That's results.

According to recent research, most Christians in this country live virtually identical lives to non-Christians. We watch the same TV programs and movies, experience divorce at about the same rates as the secular culture, and have become accommodating to a fault. As a result, we've lost any real reason for the world to become attracted to or intrigued with us.

In this sense, marketing has been forced to plug a hole that supernatural power and authority used to fill.

Compromising Our Identity

In the book *Biblical Perspectives on Evangelism: Living in a Three Storied Universe*, theologian Walter Brueggemann comments on the Old Testament nation of Israel's accommodation:

> In the disciplines of fasting and sackcloth, the Israelites "separated themselves from all foreigners" and confessed their sin (Nehemiah 9:1-2). This act in the drama needs to be understood carefully. Wrongly understood, according to Christian stereotypes of Jews, this separation sounds like arrogant legalism. Such a view misses the point completely. Rather, this community in its amnesia had assimilated itself, domesticated its memory, and compromised its identity, so that it had nothing left of itself. Judaism had become such a detrimental embarrassment, that Jews had worked to overcome their Jewishness. And now, in these dangerous liturgical acts, Jews are facing up to their oddity, to their strong commitment, to their distinctive obedience. The recovery of distinctiveness entails the acceptance of an odd identity.

> I report this point to you because I believe the church in the United States faces a crisis of accommodation and compromise that is near to final evaporation. Note well, the distinctiveness is not in doctrine or in morality, but in memory. For the text adds that all through this time of separation, "They stood up in their place and read from the book of the law."[17]

Remember the *Unique Selling Proposition*—what makes a product different from every other product in the marketplace. What makes the Church different and unique today?

Hopefully, it's more than the snappy design of your church newsletter.

Understand and Deal with the Tension of the Marketing Conflict

The Christian life is hard, there's no doubt about it. People who gave up everything to follow Christ have been burned at the stake, crucified upside down, boiled alive, dismembered, imprisoned and disgraced. Today, we live in the most democratic and free society in the history of the Church, but that freedom has lulled us into cultural accommodation. As a result, we've lost our focus on the hard sayings of Jesus and tried to refocus on what God supposedly says about buying a Mercedes, owning a private jet or having a coffee bar at church.

Don't get me wrong. None of these things are inherently evil or immoral. I stand for hours in security lines at airports dreaming about owning a private jet. But I worry that we've so strongly bought into the American way of life that we've become more identified with capitalism and democracy than with faith. As we've grown in political power, we're becoming known as the people who are *against* everything instead of the people who are *for* something. We've become the "Christian Right," with a perception that our greatest goal is to push everyone around.

Have we lost our moral authority in the culture by trading it in for a larger network TV audience?

Is there an answer? If you look deeply into the issue, I really don't think so, which is exactly why the marketing conflict exists. We can plead a life of poverty until we realize that reaching a mass audience through the media costs millions of dollars. We can make a hard stand for an issue until we realize that without some negotiation we'll never have much influence in government. We can be strident about public morality until we come up against other belief systems that want an equal voice in the conversation. As Brueggemann points out, the Jewish nation wrestled with the divisive issue of cultural accommodation thousands of years ago, so this is nothing new.

That doesn't cause us to stop, but it does make us aware of the tension involved in presenting our message to a twenty-first-century audience.

Financial challenges are a great example. Pastor Gary Keesee in Columbus, Ohio, was a financial planner before he was called into ministry. From that unique perspective he likes to say, "You'll never achieve your destiny until you get the money thing fixed." For instance, just try to walk away from your job and be a missionary with a huge financial debt hanging over your head, or attempt to go into full-time ministry with a poor record balancing a budget. Without a miracle, you're in for a real challenge.

Life happens. As fallen creatures, we live in conflict every day. But many refuse to accept the conflict. On the one hand, some Christian marketing "experts" relentlessly extol the virtues of marketing churches and ministries with little regard for the damage it can cause. On the other hand, academics and ministry leaders have written carloads of books decrying marketing as the end of the church as we know it.

Meanwhile, somewhere in the middle, I wrestle with the task of getting the Christian message to as many people as possible, and at the same time, keeping the church distinctive and unique without making us look weird and crazy.

The conflict will always be there. Our goal is to seek balance. We want to get people into the seats without harming the integrity or perception of the church as a life-changing entity, and yet extend grace to those who walk away in spite of our best efforts.

Academics or critics can sit at a distance and make their pronouncements, but for those of us in the trenches, wrestling with that conflict is a way of life.

CHAPTER NINE

THE BRANDING IMPERATIVE

A generation ago the question was, "What is truth?"
Today, the question is, "What's the point?"
BILLY GRAHAM

Branding is not foolproof, and it's not a magic bullet. In the secular world, the most brilliant advertising campaign can't make a bad product a success; and in the religious world, branding can't cover up serious ministry mistakes or hypocrisy. Moral failure, bad management or spiritual apathy cannot be "fixed" by a great brand. Integrity matters.

Real branding is about creating and maintaining trust; and without delivery on that trust, the relationship is broken. A number of years ago I was asked to create a new brand for a national ministry client. It was a perfect situation. The ministry leader was articulate, driven to excellence and committed, and he had a powerful message to share. As a result, we created a new look and feel for the ministry, designed a powerful identity and were able to unify that look and feel throughout the ministry's television outreach, website, print materials, and more.

But we quickly discovered a problem: customer service. The client organization had a corrupt computer database of supporters, so I immediately brought in an expert at analyzing and evaluating those types of data-related problems. Normally, it was not a big deal, but the first challenge we encountered was a ministry team that cared little about customer service.

As a result, they refused to acknowledge the corrupted data, and in a futile attempt to save face, spent months denying it was an issue. But because we refused to let go, they finally were forced to admit there was a problem, and it was significant indeed.

People would purchase products from the ministry and wait months to receive them. They would make donations without receiving a thank-you or further follow-up. First-time donors were dropped out of the system without being encouraged to become regular givers. Worse, John Q. Public from Tulsa was getting John Q. Public from Cleveland's product orders and vice versa.

It was a nightmare.

It took more than a year to resolve the crisis, partly because of the level of corruption in the file, and partly because of the intransigence of the staff. They refused to act on the problem for fear of looking inept, and then they refused to believe it was serious until it was too late.

At that one ministry alone, I calculated that they lost millions of dollars in potential donations from supporters who were angry, frustrated and eventually left because of the way they were treated. One of my great frustrations with the client was how our branding changes were generating far more responses through television and the Web, but those new people would soon become so frustrated they would walk away. It's hard enough to get the phones to ring in the first place, but then allowing them to slip through your fingers is inexcusable.

You cannot put a price tag on great customer service. Don't let your calling, gifts and talents get damaged because of uncaring or unprofessional staff members. Customer service is vital in a secular business, but it's absolutely critical in religious and nonprofit work. Acquiring a new customer is five times more expensive than keeping a current customer happy. Finding new customers is more thrilling, and keeping old customers is hard work. But the truth is, you'll profit far more by keeping people than by having to constantly find new ones.

We call the places where a customer or potential supporter encounters your organization a "touch point," and it's vital that they receive the best treatment possible, no matter where they choose to encounter the ministry. Telephone operators, mailing and shipping staff, tour guides, media directors, ushers, Sunday School teachers and workers, marketing people–anyone who could possibly meet a customer, church member or supporter needs to understand just how important they are and who they represent.

Employee Evangelists

A few years ago, I was unexpectedly caught at an airport when a major snowstorm blew in. Hundreds of flights were cancelled, stranding thousands of frustrated people on the ground. The airline I was flying was a major company with thousands of employees. They had spent millions developing their brand, millions more on advertising and public relations, and had hired some of the top executives in the airline industry. But that night, for thousands of their customers, that airline wasn't represented by its CEO, its top executives or its advertising gurus; it was represented by the men and women at the ticket counter–the people on the front line.

Had they dropped the ball, no amount of advertising and branding could have fixed the perception in the mind of their customers.

Remember, your employees are the embodiment of your brand. Make every employee an evangelist for your organization. Just as a salesman at a department store represents that store to a customer, the ministry employees that your audience, supporters or congregation come in contact with are your brand.

When it comes to customer service, branding consultant Wally Olins has a list of simple rules for keeping your service up to par:

1. *Organize your operation around the brand.* In other words, get everyone in your organization talking to each other. Do you remember when you started and your team consisted of 3 or 4 people? Everyone was on the same page simply because you were probably all in the same room. But we grow and people stop talking to each other. Little kingdoms get set up around the church and ministry, and before long, people start fighting over budgets, status and who knows what else.

   In an effort to get everyone on the same page, I have some clients who have done away with titles to get rid of the inside politics and competition. Other clients provide everyone the same size office and furniture. In what I would consider an act of desperation, one major church has their leadership staff switch jobs every year or so to keep them guessing (which also keeps them, in my opinion, terrified).

   Certainly there are problems with each of these techniques, but I understand the motivation. The important thing to remember is that it's a Herculean effort to keep everyone working together without pride, or ego, rearing its ugly head. Whatever your strategy, keep people talking and focus that discussion on the brand.

2. *Train your people to live the brand.* If they don't buy into the vision, they are working against it. That's why so many companies have off-site retreats, team-building activities, training classes, and more.

3. *Behave the way you talk.* Do your people model the behavior they are supposed to be representing? Do they represent the organization well? It's one thing to be caught in a strip club when you work for a cell phone company. It's another thing altogether to be caught in a strip club while working for a church.

4. *Always remember that your staff is the brand.* A surly salesperson can forever sour you on the entire company, and an unfriendly usher can do the same.

5. *Be consistent and coherent.* Make sure the customer experience is uniform throughout the organization.

6. *Treat customers with respect.* Don't let your people get complacent. Your supporters are your lifeline and should never be taken for granted.

7. *Listen to customers' complaints.* Through personal outbound phone calls, mail or Web surveys, and other techniques, listen to people. Find out how you're doing, and get regular feedback from the people who encounter your organization the most.

8. *Lead by example from the top.* It starts with the leader, and there is no substitute for someone who can cast the vision, set a spiritual and moral example, and make the tough decisions necessary to keep the vision alive.

9. *Trust your people to live the brand.* One of the greatest challenges to successful branding is the rigid organizational chart of many companies, churches and

> ministries. Once you reach a certain size, hardcore lines of demarcation are drawn and the walls go up. As a result, the sales staff doesn't talk to the designers; accounting doesn't communicate with operations; and creative doesn't talk to the executives. Nation states get set up, kingdoms are created and the company becomes something completely inorganic and inflexible. In organizations where everyone wants to do it their way, getting a new brand identity to permeate those layers of management is nearly impossible.[1]

I understand the need for organization, and I certainly don't advocate for a flat administrative chart, but I do recommend that you carefully structure your group. Small organizations have the wonderful freedom of communication, consistency and teamwork that's often missing when the company grows.

It's warfare for hearts and minds here. For a new brand to work, take extra pains to create unity and teamwork among your people. Ask them to share how the vision is played out in their respective departments and how the brand speaks to exactly how they contribute to the bottom line.

When I produce a television special or a film, I meet individually with each department head and ask how they plan to tell the story of the movie through their respective craft. For instance, what wardrobe choices will tell the story most effectively? What lighting decisions will help make each scene tell the story? How will the makeup, editing, set design and all the other elements that make a movie tell the story from their individual perspectives?

When each employee understands how his department, craft or task fits into the brand story of your organization, you'll have a team that's firing on all cylinders and finally feels part of the process.

> *We must reject the idea—well intentioned, but dead wrong—that the primary path to greatness in the social sectors is to become "more like a business."*
>
> **JIM COLLINS, AUTHOR OF *GOOD TO GREAT***

When Business and Ministry Collide

The idea that a church, ministry or nonprofit must run like a business has gained enormous momentum in the last two decades. The world is exploding with business books by a variety of gurus and supposed experts, and as a result, business thinking has become accepted dogma in religious organizations. I've always been an advocate of this development, because over the years, after working with more than 1,000 churches and ministries worldwide, I've discovered that religious organizations are often the worst run operations on the planet.

Much of that difficulty comes from the tension between performance and loyalty. Naturally, in a religious organization, profit isn't the bottom line, and therefore, performance isn't as emphasized as much as it should be. As a result, churches and ministries are filled with wonderful but incompetent people. These employees and volunteers are committed to the organization, have integrity and are good people, but they've often been promoted through the years because of loyalty rather than expertise.

I know of one major church with a single employee that I've estimated costs the organization at least $100,000 per year through sheer incompetence. She's responsible for the marketing efforts of the church but she misses print and advertising deadlines, makes costly mistakes in product shipping, doesn't know how to evaluate advertising campaigns, and her decisions on any number of issues is usually wrong. She has no experience in marketing but was promoted to the position after being a loyal and capable assistant to the pastor for many years.

Employees of one church on the West Coast actually have a rather sick joke that to be fired, you'd have to show up at a shopping mall with a machine gun and shoot a few people. A job in that organization is pretty much a job for life, no matter how poorly you might perform any given position. The lack of competence, poor stewardship and resulting mismanagement of the congregation's money boggles the mind.

In another major ministry, poor management created an atmosphere of insecurity and terror throughout the organization. One incompetent senior ministry executive spent years managing employees through fear disguised as concern. For instance, when an employee would make a mistake, he would sit them down, express compassion and then tell them, "I'm really worried that the pastor will find out about this. If that happens, he'll fire you for sure." Much like Absalom at the city gate, he would pretend to be concerned about people but, in reality, he was buying their loyalty and using fear to undermine the pastor.

Completely unknown to the pastor, this manager was terrorizing people and pointing the finger at *him*. When I discovered the problem and shared my assessment with the pastor, he completely denied the possibility. He couldn't imagine that his employees were afraid of him, and he flatly refused to believe it. But I asked him to spend a few weeks "walking through the factory," casually spending time with employees, gaining their confidence and listening to them.

Sure enough, during my next visit a month later, he pulled me aside and said that I was right. Employees of the ministry were terrified of him and thought he ruled with an iron hand. He eventually fired the senior executive, but it took years to completely repair the damage and change the perceptions of his employees.

Spend time with employees and volunteers—that means listening time, not just talking time.

Speaking of walking through the factory, let me share one of the most important secrets of managing a successful church or ministry: Spend time with employees and volunteers. Whenever we brand a ministry, it's critical to understand the thinking of your people; and the only way to do it is to listen. You'd probably be surprised at the number of corporate executives, church pastors and nonprofit leaders who rarely spend time with employees or volunteers. I know some that haven't visited sections of the building in years.

In some cases, ministry leaders spend little or no time with the media directors, graphic designers or writing staff—the very people who are the key to presenting that leader to a national media audience. They rarely hear him express his heart or have close contact, and then the leader wonders why he's not happy with the way he's being presented on national television or radio.

Don't automatically assume that everyone is on board with your vision or the direction of the new brand identity. It's critical that they feel you have their interests in mind, that you are listening and that you share their concerns.

Helping People Change

Having branded some of the major ministries in America, we're not oblivious to the fact that many employees or team members will either disagree with our approach or actively resist it. To a point, this is good. We certainly don't have all the answers; and a vibrant, relevant organization is one where disagreements happen, ideas are debated and directions are discussed.

But some organizations are paralyzed because they can't move from vibrant debate to unified action. To prepare you for potential disagreement, here are some of the key reasons why people resist change.

1. Love of Routine

My father adores IHOP (the International House of Pancakes) and would eat there any time, any place. On the other side of the family, before my father-in-law passed away, he wouldn't think of touching a meal until he had a slice of bread with it. If the waiter brought the bread late, he would let his meal get cold before he would eat it.

Millions of people only fly on one airline, only drive a Chevy, get dressed in a certain order, can't function without that first cup of coffee. To do any of these things otherwise would drive them nuts.

I'm not a geneticist, so I don't know if it's our wiring or something we've acquired. All I know is that many people are slaves to routines that help them understand life, feel comfortable or make sense of things.

In many organizations, breaking work-related routines will chill some employees to the bone, so be ready for a fight. The key in these situations is pointing out the *new* routine and how it will make their life better, generate more income, increase the bottom line, expand ministry, or whatever.

Years ago, I worked with a cameraman who couldn't function on location without a printed schedule. Whenever we changed the shooting plan or began to improvise, we would literally see him begin to sweat and get nervous. In those cases, I had our production manager create a fictional schedule, and although it meant absolutely nothing, he could hold it in his hand and feel like we had a direction and purpose for the day. The world was fine for him once again.

2. Potential Embarrassment and Survival

Change is often perceived as an unfair encroachment on a person's territory, and he or she worries about failing or looking bad—especially to superiors. This is understandable, but it's absolutely necessary that ministry employees comprehend that *change does not mean they've been doing something wrong*. This is not about mistakes; it's about responding to the changing culture with a fresh, new approach. We want everyone to embrace the change, take ownership of it and help us make it happen. A successful re-branding is something that happens from the inside.

That's why it's critically important to present the new branding effort in a positive light. It's not happening because we've screwed up; it's happening because we want to become more effective and move to the next level.

3. Miscommunication or Lack of Trust

What people don't understand, they will often resist. We must be clear about the change—why we're doing this, and how we're doing this. No one should feel left out; and we need to encourage his or her ideas and suggestions. This is an exciting time for the ministry, and we need to enjoy the possibilities.

After my first meeting with one ministry, a key member of the media team abruptly quit his position. I didn't understand it, and on a future visit, I asked his wife, who worked in another department, about it. Her response was unexpected: "Well, Bob assumed that with the changes you want to make, he'll probably get fired anyway, so he decided the best thing to do was to go ahead and resign."

Amazing. I had no intention of firing him, but he was so misinformed and lacked trust in the ministry's ability to do the right thing that he purposely cut himself out of what became one of our most successful branding experiences.

4. Differing Ways of Evaluating Success

Because of their limited perspective, some employees may see the cost as greater than the benefits. There will always be people who are comfortable in their current situation, so the risk of change makes them extremely nervous. There certainly are financial costs related to change, but the cost in not changing can be catastrophic.

This is normally a case of limited vision for those outside the leadership team. While the leaders can see the big picture, we have to remember that employees in the media, missions, accounting, education or even the mailing and shipping departments may not have the same view. It's vital that we keep them informed and help them understand the scale we're using to evaluate success.

5. Poor Experiences with Previous Organizations

Sometimes I encounter an employee who went through a similar but badly executed experience in a previous organization. People were fired without cause; dramatic changes were thrust on employees without notice; or the creative strategy was flawed. As a result, they witnessed the disaster firsthand, and now they react reflexively in the negative when anything similar comes up.

The best solution here is taking the time to present the case for change and allowing employees to buy in to the process. Once they see the potential and understand the process of change, they begin to support the vision.

Always remember that when people think that something is their idea, they will fight to the death to make it happen. Don't dictate to your team; allow them to take ownership. President Ronald Reagan was right when he said the famous line, "There's no limit to what a man can accomplish, as long as it doesn't matter who gets the credit."

While working for one major media ministry, it didn't take me long to realize the evangelist wanted people to think everything was his idea. So it didn't take long for me to start planting ideas in his head before the meetings. I would suggest alternate approaches, drop seeds of ideas in casual conversation and make recommendations to him privately where no one else could hear.

Sure enough, usually on a three-day cycle, during production meetings, he would regurgitate my ideas as his own. But I discovered that when he thought the idea was his, he would do anything to make it work. It didn't bother me that he took the credit, because at least we were making good ideas happen.

6. Lack of Confidence in Management or in the Decision-Making Process

People don't believe that all the relevant information has been included in the process; something must be left out. Leadership expert John Maxwell teaches that an effective leader can and often should make a decision when he has at least 65 percent of the information he needs. Some executives put off changes, thinking, *If I just had one more piece of information* . . . Like rearranging deck chairs on the Titanic, we can keep discussing and waiting for more information while the organization slowly loses influence in the culture and eventually crashes around us.

Financial Results or Mission?

Change needs to happen in the church today, but because of the reasons people resist change, and other issues, reaching the point of positive change can be extraordinarily difficult. As a result, I spent years trying to translate solid business and leadership practices into church and nonprofit life. Certainly, in many cases, better management, organizational structure, discipline and techniques made a significant difference. There's no substitute for productivity, no matter what your goals, and much of the current business and leadership thinking can apply directly to challenges we face in the church and nonprofit world.

However, the more I worked with religious organizations and nonprofits, the more I realized there was a side effect as a result of the business principles I was teaching. In some cases, the techniques didn't get the same results they would have produced in a secular company; and in others, I was worried that we were turning pastors and nonprofit leaders into entrepreneurs who were more concerned about *bottom line* thinking than *mission* thinking.

Certainly, as I and others advocated better leadership, more disciplined organizational structure, accountability and more effective management techniques over the years, we began to see a much more professional attitude in many churches and ministries. Employee performance tightened up, finances were used more effectively, ministries became more effective, outreaches expanded, and the perception about the organizations improved in the local community.

However, I also began to notice other, more disturbing signs. I watched pastors transform themselves into corporate executives. I saw church and ministry managers become PDA zombies, walking through the day with their eyes glued to their incoming email, and a corporate mentality that prioritized financial results over mission.

Recently, on a visit to a large church, I spent the day with the pastor, evaluating and advising on media ministry issues. But from the time the pastor picked me up at the hotel for breakfast until he dropped me off late that night after the evening service, he was held in bondage to his PDA. Literally every 10 minutes he would glance at his email as if driven by some strange voodoo spell. During the day, we attended planning meetings with his top-level staff, attended a youth service and even looked in on a family during a counseling session. But no matter how intimate, serious or critical the moment, he continually allowed himself to be interrupted by the "ding" of an incoming email message.

I wanted to rip it out of his hand and scream at him that human contact was far more important than those little digital messages!

The executive mentality expresses itself in other ways as well:

- Pastors with schedules so busy they have little time for real human contact
- Hiring outside "professionals" for the kinds of church jobs that used to be driven by volunteers with a personal passion for ministry
- The substitution of software training for people skills
- A relentless drive for results instead of mission
- An overall attitude of structure that kills the loving attitude of fellowship (ushers forcing you to sit in certain places, high security systems, controlled access to certain areas of the church, the entourage of assistants [bodyguards?] that escort the pastor out of his car, into his office, onto the platform and back to his car again unmolested)

Certainly in a mega-church world, caution is in order. High-level security systems to protect children's areas are simply a necessary part of the culture now; and there's no question that with expensive computer, sound and lighting equipment, security is important. And it's impossible for each member of a church of 1,000 or more people to have all the private time he or she wants with the pastor.

But in the midst of these advances, I began to see "mission drift" in certain organizations when the focus went from community to commodity. When things and results generated the same concern and value as people, I saw a distinct shift in the direction of pastors and ministry leaders.

Bookshelves in pastors' offices that had previously been filled with volumes on theology, Church history and doctrine have been replaced by the latest bestsellers on business motivation and sales.

That's when I discovered a small monograph by Jim Collins, author of the business classic *Good to Great: Why Some Companies Make the Leap and Others Don't*. Apparently, Collins had been wrestling with many of the same issues in the nonprofit world, including groups like museums, youth programs and school outreaches, as well as churches. As a result, he wanted to adapt many of the "good to great" principles he'd discussed in his book; but this time, he focused on the social (or nonprofit and religious) sector of the economy.

Since the monograph was intended to be an addition to the book, he called it *Good to Great in the Social Sectors*. In it, he realized that businesses and nonprofit organizations were two different types of entities, and the same principles that drive one do not necessarily work for the other. He realized the distinction wasn't about business or social:

> That's when it dawned on me: we need a new language. The critical distinction isn't between business and social, but between great and good. We need to reject the naïve imposition of the "language of business" on

> the social sectors, and instead, jointly embrace a language of greatness.[2]

Collins realized that trying to implement business principles in a church, ministry or other nonprofit organization does not work, because while business is driven by *financial returns*, a nonprofit is driven by *mission*. In other words, a business that doesn't make money is a loser, but nonprofits are "non-profit" by nature. Although we'd love it if we had all the money we needed, for most churches and ministries–even in an age of prosperity preaching–that's not what we're about, and it's not why we exist.

The Distinctives of Churches and Nonprofit Ministries

In the executive-driven world of many pastors, that critical distinction gets lost. But what does this mean for branding a typical church or ministry?

Driven by Meaning

Businesses are often driven by money, but nonprofit employees are driven by meaning. I'm certainly an advocate of paying people what they're worth when possible, but in most applications, nonprofits just can't compete with the salary scale of corporations. So instead of constantly worrying that you can't afford good employees, shift your search to people looking for meaning. They're out there, and they want to make a difference. If you have a strong vision and a compelling mission, chances are, there are people willing to work for a fraction of the money in order to be part of a greater project in life. Meaning is a powerful part of your brand, so keep the vision in front of the people, and keep it alive.

Results Quantified by the Mission

It's easy for a business to evaluate financial returns and product sales, but it's much more difficult for a church or ministry to quantify the results of mission. Working with gangs, feeding the homeless, evangelism, youth work, medical clinics, spiritual development, family counseling, teaching and training—these are much more difficult to apply to a chart and track progress, but it can be done.

In the old days, national ministries like those of Billy Graham, Oral Roberts and others kept detailed records of men and women converted at their meetings. They were very careful about recording that information and keeping it in front of their supporters and employees. I've personally read through thousands of the handwritten cards filled out by men and women at Oral Roberts's tent crusades back in the forties and fifties. Those men knew the value of quantifying their mission—not from an ego perspective but from the perspective of evaluating the results and staying on track.

Begin working with your leadership team to set benchmarks for mission. Fund-raising and product sales will always be important, but fund-raising results will always be more difficult without mission results.

Diversified Funding

With a business, income results from the sale of widgets. Certainly investment income, tax strategy, long-term planning and other policies play important roles, but the primary engine that drives corporate funding is sales. However, with a nonprofit, funding often comes from a wide variety of sources: individual tithing, large donors, grants, fellowships, partnership, product sales, capital campaigns, and more.

One of the constant challenges for nonprofits is funding, and the most successful ministry leaders are the men and women who understand the importance of casting a wide net. As Collins puts it, "The critical question is not 'How much money do we make?' but 'How can we develop a sustainable resource engine to deliver superior performance relative to our mission?'"

One of the issues most church leaders miss is the need to sustain a fund-raising program for the long haul. Very often, particularly in media ministry, an incredible moment will come when, due to TV exposure, a bestselling book, a news story or other convergence of events, the ministry is immediately and dramatically launched into the national spotlight. As a result, the website experiences millions of hits, book sales skyrocket or record donations come in through TV or direct mail.

When that happens, it's wonderful serendipity, and we thank God for it. But if the church or ministry doesn't have a financial plan for the long haul, sooner or later, it's back to oblivion. Time after time I've seen ministries given the remarkable gift of unintended publicity but then drop the ball for a lack of cohesive, long-term financial strategy.

Resource Funding Means Far More than Money

Many churches in this country have amassed an army of volunteers to accomplish remarkable work, an example being the enormous response by churches after Hurricane Katrina. When the government botched the job early on, it was churches and ministries that stood in the gap and supplied much needed help and relief. Certainly that response took a significant financial commitment, but what made the real difference was thousands of Christian volunteers helping the recovery efforts.

Facing the Giants

All of this isn't to say that financial partnerships don't work in the nonprofit sector. The African-American church community has been especially innovative in harnessing the power of local businesses to extend their outreach and work. Obviously, caution is in order when churches become landlords and business owners, and we have to go to great lengths to keep our focus on mission; but when it works, it can make a strong statement to the culture.

Pastor Michael Catt of Sherwood Baptist Church in Albany, Georgia, motivated by church media director Alex Kendrick, encouraged his church members to produce, act and market a feature motion picture. *Facing the Giants*, a touching story about a year in the life of a Christian high school football coach and his team, received so much attention that Sony Pictures picked it up for distribution in theaters nationwide. Thanks to the massive volunteer contribution of its members, they were able to produce the picture for a budget of only $100,000, and it made millions at the box office and DVD sales.

Can a local church impact the entire country?

Absolutely.

Whatever the engine is that drives your funding, without a clear, cohesive brand identity, it will be very tough to instill the kind of motivation in donors, volunteers or partners to make your vision happen.

It's the brand that helps you gain momentum, because it's rarely the one-time spark or brilliant campaign that generates major income but rather the long-term, steady, day-by-day strategy of forward movement. When your identity conveys an image of confidence, vision, commitment and determination, it's far easier to motivate people to make that vision happen, because, as Collins says, people love winners.

That's because brand identity is all about trust. When your congregation, ministry partners, supporters or audience trust you with their financial resources, funding happens. But it must be conveyed through a clear identity, integrity and solid reputation.

Understand the Difference in Leadership

One thing Jim Collins makes clear is that business leadership is often quite different from nonprofit leadership. He calls it the difference between "executive" and "legislative" leadership. In a business—particularly a privately owned company—the chief executive drives the train. He or she makes the decisions; and at least from an authoritative point of view, those decisions are the bottom line.

But in most nonprofits, particularly in a church or ministry setting, leadership involves building coalitions, assembling teams, and practicing bilateral cooperation. This book isn't a treatise on leadership, but it's important to realize the difference. Growing up as a pastor's son in a small church in Charlotte, North Carolina, I watched from the front row as my father had to deal with the elder board, church committees, deacons and other influential members in order to make decisions happen. He became an expert at building coalitions and "working the room."

Today, particularly in independent churches and ministries, I often see more executive-style leadership, and this isn't necessarily a bad thing. In a nonprofit founded by a single person with a clear, unified vision, a board usually exists, but it's often little more than an advisory group, especially when the ministry is built around the testimony or calling of a particular person. Sometimes this happens when the organization begins as a small mom-and-pop ministry and, over a period of years, grows into a national outreach.

There are a couple of different viewpoints on the issue, and this isn't the place for that discussion. I do believe that a visionary leader of a church or ministry shouldn't be held back by an obstinate board or by disgruntled church members. If God has chosen this person for a leadership role, I'll usually default to their decisions. Especially when accountability measures are in place, I'm often comfortable giving them wider latitude in church or ministry leadership.

But I've also seen latitude horribly abused by egotistical leaders who live lives of moral compromise under the auspices of "prophetic vision." They get a bit too used to the power, prestige and financial incentives of national ministry leadership, and they use their position as ruler more than leader. Some, of course, have caused great damage to the faith through moral, financial or leadership abuse.

The key to balance is to understand that in most ministry situations, we can't simply copy leadership from a business perspective. When legislative leadership is required, we need to understand the difference and act accordingly. Granted, many leadership experts will say that part of being true leaders is to understand the difference and respond appropriately; and with that, I would agree.

The Ability to Deliver

A final word on the issue of leadership in the nonprofit sector has to do with your ability to deliver on your promise. Whether you raise money for building water wells in Africa, pregnancy clinics in Cleveland, gang intervention in Los Angeles or evangelism to Eastern Europe, you have to accomplish the mission for your organization to continue.

Earlier I mentioned that you can't brand a lie. You can't create a brand identity around a specific mission and never show results. People will follow you for a time, but sooner or later they start asking questions. Granted, experience has shown us that the Christian television audience is quite gullible, and millions of dollars have been donated to questionable causes, flawed theology, bad teaching and evangelists with questionable morals (not to mention really bad hair). But over the long haul, building your ministry through results is the key to success.

Creating that mindshare with your support base cannot be overestimated. Jim Collins gives the following example of how the power of a brand is the key to building a great identity:

> Does Harvard truly deliver a better education and do better academic work than other universities? Perhaps, but the emotional pull of Harvard overcomes any doubt when it comes to raising funds. Despite having an endowment in excess of $20 billion, donations continue to flow. As one Harvard graduate put it, 'I give money to Harvard every year, and sometimes I feel like I'm bringing sand to the beach.' Does the Red Cross truly do the best job of disaster relief? Perhaps, but the brand reputation of the Red Cross gives people an easy answer to the question, 'How can I help?' when a disaster hits. Is the American Cancer Society the best mechanism for conquering cancer, or the Nature Conservancy the most effective at protecting the environment? Perhaps, but their brand reputations give people an easy way to support a cause they care about. The same applies to government-funded entities. NYPD has a brand. The United States Marine Corps has a brand. NASA has a brand. Anyone seeking to cut funding must contend with the brand.[3]

Brand Equity

This type of identity leads us to the issue of "brand equity." In this case, the term "equity" isn't about money; it's about the "savings account" you've built with your brand in the minds of your customers. Once the mindshare with your customer or audience is created, you can begin to deepen the relationship to new levels. Media researcher Erik Du Plessis describes it as "the number of people who will buy the brand with the 'least thinking.'"[4] The customer has no concerns, and very little mental discussion, about the purchase. It's like a "brand memory" built from years of positive feelings about the product, person or institution.

In the religious world, the Billy Graham Evangelistic Association (BGEA) has enormous brand equity when it comes to fulfilling its mission. As a result of years of ministry achievement around the world, millions of lives touched and enormous integrity, BGEA has created extremely positive feelings from its supporters and the general public as well. With that kind of brand equity, an organization can weather very difficult times and still retain a positive relationship with the public.

Brand equity isn't just about overcoming scandal, poor sales or some other disaster. Brand equity makes marketing easier because it's far easier to sell the brand. In other words, you're building on the fact that people already know you, like you and want a relationship with you. In advertising there are two main thrusts: current or past customers, and new potential customers. Brand equity helps most with current or past customers, because it helps overcome obstacles or hesitation to repurchase. When they already trust the brand, you don't have to spend the time, money and effort telling customers who you are, what you're about and how you or your product can change their life.

Does Anyone Really Watch TV Anymore?

In my years of producing programs, I've discovered that few people really watch TV in the sense of sitting there focused solely on the screen. In today's world of multitasking, people are more likely to do something else while they're also watching your program. My wife irons clothes while she watches TV, and I'm usually catching up on magazine reading.

I discovered this phenomenon years ago when I saw the Woody Allen movie *Zelig* in the theater. *Zelig* was filmed in a mock documentary style and was based on the fictional story of a man who wanted to blend in with the crowd so much that he actually transformed himself into the types of people he was with at any given time. Thus, when he was with African-American jazz musicians, he morphed into an African-American jazz musician; when he was in a hospital, he transformed like a chameleon into a member of the hospital staff. His emotional desire to fit in was so great that his physical body somehow followed suit.

It was a wonderful fable about how badly people want to fit into society. I liked the movie so much that when it came out on video, we invited two other couples over one night to see the film. But the moment I put the video into the player, something strange happened. Instead of getting everyone's rapt attention, my wife popped up and said, "I'll go and fix dessert for everyone." One of the other wives followed her into the kitchen to help. Then another one pulled out some knitting needles, her husband reached for a magazine and the final guy picked up a book.

Exasperated, I stood up and said, "Hey, I wanted you to watch this movie!" They all looked at me like I had lost my mind and said, "We *are* watching the movie."

At that moment, I realized that's the way people watch TV today. No one really sits there focused on the screen. Most people are eating, getting dressed, playing around with a hobby or doing something else.

It wasn't long before I noticed that when I travel, after I check into my hotel room, the first thing I do is turn on the TV.

I have no plans to actually watch it, but apparently I like the room noise—my little video friend in the corner. Television has become the background noise of our lives, and we watch it in spurts and grab snatches of it on the fly.

Perhaps that's the most unique thing of all about television. We actually comprehend it without watching. We can work in another room, only passing by the set periodically, read a magazine, or talk with friends, but we're still able to track with much of the programming.

Read the following email I received the other day:

Aoccdrnig to rsceearh at an Elingsh uinervtisy, it deosn't mttaer in waht oredr the ltteers in a wrod are, the olny iprmoatnt tihng is taht the frist and lsat ltteers are in the rghit pclae. The rset can be a toatl mses and you can sitll raed it wouthit a porbelm. This is bcuseae we do not raed ervey lteter by itslef but the wrod as a wlohe.

That strange little exercise was designed to show how the brain works when it comes to reading. It's not the detailed spelling that really matters. We apparently grab words in groups and understand them in the context of the actual sentence.

It's not much different when viewing television. We don't often watch TV to the exclusion of any other distraction, but we can still grab enough meaning to make sense of the program.

But that also means that producers and brands need to become better at cutting through the clutter of people's lives to get their attention to make sure that meaning happens. If people are multitasking through life, we need to make our programs stand out enough to capture their attention and refocus them toward our vision.

How Much Do We Remember?

The onslaught of advertising messages we receive every day means that we don't remember much, and in that environment, a strong brand is more important than ever to the success of a product. In the battle with media clutter, religious media is losing, simply because of the overwhelming odds. In *The Advertised Mind*, Erik Du Plessis reports that audiences in countries with the lowest number of commercial messages during programs actually remember far more about those commercials. In Denmark for instance, viewers are exposed to an average of 200 commercials a week; in the United States, exposure climbs to nearly 1,000 per week; and in Japan, the amount of exposure is even more.[5]

I'm talking about TV commercials only–not print ads, radio, billboards or Internet advertising.

In Denmark, audiences remember far more about the commercials than in the U.S. or Japan, because in the latter countries, the incredible wave of clutter makes it difficult to remember anything with accuracy. In addition, according to Du Plessis, the ability to remember commercials drops with each passing year. In 1965 for instance, 18 percent of viewers in the United States remembered the last commercial they saw on television. By 1981, however, that number had dropped to 7 percent, and by 1990 it had plummeted to only 4 percent. He reports that in West Germany, where fewer spots are broadcast, people's ability to remember commercials only dropped from 18 percent to 14 percent between the years 1985 and 1989.[6]

In spite of the millions of dollars spent on commercials in America, and the brilliant, creative minds developing the advertising, it's the swamp of media clutter that becomes the sticking point. In this environment, a strong brand is essential, because a product or organization needs the equity of a memorable identity to cut through the disorder and muddle of the maze of advertising the audience is confronted with on a daily basis.

Smashing the Brand

Shortly after the turn of the last century, a designer named Earl R. Dean was working at the Root Glass Company and was given an assignment to design a soft drink bottle that could accomplish two things.

First, it could be recognized in the dark. Simply by touching the bottle, the customer would know the brand of soft drink almost instinctively.

Second, even if the bottle was smashed to pieces, the customer could pick up any broken shard and still tell at first glance what the drink had been.

Dean first went for inspiration to the cocoa bean pod, which had contours that were unlike any soft drink bottle on the market. Then, after a great deal of design and development, he unveiled what has become known as the Coca-Cola contourization strategy that used shape to express the brand.

The classic Coke bottle has become one of the most famous icons ever designed and is recognized in virtually every country on the planet. Even today, after plenty of competitors have long since gone out of business, the Coke bottle is still in service, proving the power of the "smash test."

Thousands of companies today use the smash test to evaluate their brands. In other words, if your logo was removed from the product, would the colors, graphics or other distinctive images still express the brand? Even better, how much could you smash your organization and still have it reflect your brand? Is your brand so much a part of your organization's DNA that every single aspect of your business reflects the brand?

Branding isn't just a matter of brochures and website designs. It's the story of your organization expressed through customer service, building design, uniforms, procedures and policies, employee training, and much more.

Getting Back to the Core

On Saturday, February 24, 2006, the *Wall Street Journal* reported on the contents of a nearly 800-word internal memo written by Starbucks chairman Howard Schultz to his employees. At the time, Starbucks had grown to 13,000 locations, with the goal of establishing 40,000 locations around the globe. Reminding employees that "success is not an entitlement," Schultz was concerned about the growing competition from other fast-food restaurants that had begun going head to head with Starbucks in coffee sales.

But his real focus was the fear of losing the Starbucks story on the global journey toward massive growth. In recent years, the company had begun switching to automatic espresso machines, allowing the coffee to be served faster and eliminating the need to grind beans or pull espresso shots by hand. In their efforts to increase speed and efficiency, Schultz wondered if they had lost much of the romance and theater of the Starbucks coffee experience.

The new automatic machines blocked the sight line, so the customer had lost the ability to interact with the barista to see their beverage being made and, without grinding, they lost the sensory experience of smelling the fresh roasted beans. Mr. Schultz described it as "the loss of aroma–perhaps the most powerful nonverbal signal we had in our stores."

Howard Schultz knows it's about having a great coffee experience and that perhaps in pursuit of modernization and efficiency that core element of the brand was being lost.

What have you lost in the pursuit of expansion and growth? Growth is a wonderful thing, but be very careful what you sacrifice to reach your goals. Brand equity and customer trust are extremely difficult to earn, so be very careful how you grow.

CHAPTER TEN

THE FUTURE OF BRANDING FAITH

The moment you begin to think of yourself as great, your slide toward mediocrity will have already begun.
JIM COLLINS, AUTHOR OF *GOOD TO GREAT*

In times of change, learners inherit the earth, while the learned find themselves beautifully equipped to deal with a world that no longer exists.
ERIC HOFFER, SOCIAL PHILOSOPHER

During 2007, while directing and producing a feature documentary film called *The Better Hour,* on the life and work of British Parliamentarian William Wilberforce, I discovered that one of the first and most well-known images of the eighteenth-century abolitionist movement in England was a brand. The focus of the brand was a medallion featuring the image of a kneeling African man.

William Wilberforce had struggled for more than a decade to end the slave trade throughout the British Empire. As a member of Parliament, he had argued, debated, organized and tried everything in his power to change the thinking of the English populace on the issue, but his struggle continued.

Driven by his Christian faith, and supported by his friend John Newton, former slave trader himself, and writer of the classic hymn "Amazing Grace," he pressed on, trying to make the public aware that they should view slavery as the evil it really was and make an historic change throughout the world.

But the slavery business was the largest industry in the Empire. Some scholars today equate the financial impact to England of its loss would have been similar to the loss of the defense industry in America today. The forces for continuing the trade were massive and powerful throughout the country.

Growing ever more frustrated, Wilberforce commissioned Josiah Wedgewood, creator of the legendary pottery and china, to design a medallion "expressive of an African in chains in a supplicating posture." The words surrounding the nearly naked man were engraved as a motto: Am I Not A Man And A Brother?

Strategically, the phrase was designed to appeal to both Christians and secularists, and it made an immediate impression on British society. In 1788, an order of the cameos was shipped to Benjamin Franklin in Philadelphia, and wearing the cameo became a fashion statement for abolitionists and antislavery sympathizers in the United States. They were worn as jewelry of all kinds and were mounted like pictures on walls in homes. They also adorned hair combs and snuffboxes.

The general public was enthralled, and the image started to appear in major pamphlets of the day. The goal was to focus public opinion on the slave trade, and it worked. Before long, the momentum changed the debate in Parliament, and Wilberforce and his supporters finally won the day.

The medallion had done what years of debate, intellectual discussion and governmental action could not do alone. It had helped change the culture and had ended the slave trade in the British Empire.

When a powerful story and indelible image is connected to a person, cause, product or organization, anything can happen.

> *There is a simple way to package information that, under the right circumstances, can make it irresistible. All you have to do is find it.*
>
> **MALCOLM GLADWELL, *THE TIPPING POINT*[1]**

As you can probably tell, I'm not a dogmatic prophet who believes it's my way or the highway. I have more at stake at this than the occasional book or lecture, and I certainly have more on the line than many writers on the subject. As a working professional in the media industry, I have major church, ministry and nonprofit clients needing precise information right now, so I'm constantly learning, growing and experimenting with new styles, methods and techniques to accomplish their vision. Essentially, I am a media activist, calling the Church to a better understanding of how media is influencing our society, and how to use the media to share a message of hope with the culture.

Branding isn't an exact science. It's organic, reflecting the changing culture, trends and ideas of each generation.

I do know that the media and entertainment industries are undergoing massive change, and if we're not on the cusp of that change, our message will continue to be perceived as more and more out of touch and dated. Feminists, gender activists, multiculturalists, environmentalists, antiwar protesters, political bloggers, conservatives, liberals, unions, corporations, and more, are understanding the power of creating a media identity and using it to engage millions of people every day.

And it works.

While most of these organizations are admired for the ways they've used the media to advance their cause, we in the Christian community are for the most part still way behind the curve.

Not so long ago, we thought political power would accomplish our goals, but we realized it could backfire. We tried to shove people around with boycotts but alienated the very people we were trying to reach. We became allied with political causes and parties and estranged ourselves from the culture.

The intersection of faith and politics isn't the purpose of this book, but when it comes to branding, I wonder how far political power has really taken us. I definitely encourage Christians to vote, to be politically active and never hesitate to express their faith in the public square. But as we've taken "Christianity" into the political arena, I worry that our cause for Christ has suffered.

There's no question that the Christian faith has been most effective when it has acted as salt and light. Operating on the margins of society, we've made a great contribution to the culture, and as I've said many times, it doesn't take a scholar to note the remarkable and unparalleled contribution Christianity has made to the West throughout history.

But in what most call a postmodern and post-Christian culture, we're discovering that any power we thought we had has created a backlash. Even though they acted with the best of intentions, Christian leaders of a generation ago who made Christianity a political force are now viewed by the culture as parodies and are often referred to in condescending and humorous terms.

I'm not here to argue their accomplishments, but I am here to offer a better way to impact the culture for the future.

Reaching the next generation isn't about *political* power; it's about *branding* power. It's not about what we're *against*; it's about what we're *for*. It's not about changing the culture from the *outside*; it's about changing the culture from the *inside*.

Branding is about creating a compelling story of what the Christian faith is, what it stands for and how it can change lives.

Ultimately, it's about meaning.

The search for meaning is the most powerful force in the world. It's more powerful than politics, big business and even war. As this country becomes more and more polarized politically, the only thing that will break through that bleak wall of separation is meaning. When we can show the culture that we're not against them, that we have a compelling story, and that the story can change their circumstances, I believe they will listen.

The book *The Da Vinci Code*, written primarily as a suspenseful detective story, made outrageous claims about the origins of the Christian faith that had little or nothing to do with the actual truth. And yet, the culture bought into the story to such an extent that the book became one of the biggest sellers of all time, and the movie version experienced major box office results as well.

For many leaders in the religious community, it was the apocalypse. To see the public race in such numbers to bookstores and movie theaters to view such an obviously defective story was certainly depressing, and many reacted with understandable indignation.

But the fact is, there will always be plenty of other books and movies that scorn our religious values and offend our faith. So how should we react? Should we use our political and marketing power to boycott, protest and complain, or should we somehow engage these often-offensive entertainment projects?

Looking back since *The Da Vinci Code*'s theatrical debut and DVD release, I've been thinking about the reaction of the Christian community and what we can learn in retrospect. I'm sure you'll remember that during the last few months before its release there was a wave of indignation, frustration and anger that Sony Pictures would release a major movie that essentially put forth the premise that the Christian faith was founded on false pretenses. As I was interviewed on CNN, MSNBC, CNBC and other media outlets, I often discussed the fact that Christianity seems to be the last subject people can criticize without fear of reprisal. Can you imagine if a major studio released a movie that said Muhammad and Islam were frauds? The public would be outraged.

Recently, on a national comedy network, the producers of an edgy and controversial animated cartoon series put the network to the test and filmed scenes that disparaged both Mohammed and Jesus. And just as the producers probably expected, the network refused to show Mohammed being made fun of, and censored the scene. But with Jesus, the ridicule was just fine.

It's been an interesting period to see both the secular community and the faith community react to *The Da Vinci Code*. From the beginning, I called for a civil strategy of engagement rather than protest. But now some time has passed, and what have we learned?

Boycotts are the "nuclear option" only, and must be used carefully. As I wrote this book in Los Angeles, there was a massive nationwide boycott by the Mexican community over the issue of illegal immigration. In spite of a huge turnout, the leaders of that movement immediately began to question its success. Many worried that it created bad feelings with the public and may have done more harm than good in spite of hundreds of thousands of people that turned out across the country, and massive media coverage.

During a recent boycott of a major film studio by one of America's largest Christian denominations, the studio's sales actually went up. So we need to be careful with boycotts and use them only when absolutely necessary and with great strategic planning.

Start the conversation with the culture. It's interesting that after my appearances on most of the talk shows, non-Christian producers and staff would come up and introduce themselves, congratulate me, and say things like "Wow, I didn't know there were Christians out there who thought this way." They wanted to talk with someone about the movie but were afraid of most of the Christians who loudly disapproved of the film. We must put down our protest signs, stop bullying, reach out our hands and begin the dialogue.

Use the available resources. As *The Da Vinci Code* film was released, I was very excited about all the seminars, books, teaching materials and other resources marshaled to point people to the real truth of the Bible. Websites pointed thousands of people to some of our most brilliant scholars and leaders who provided important information to help as they shared their faith with friends and family. Even the *Los Angeles Times* reported on the incredible number of pastors who used the film as a teaching tool to share the correct information about Christianity.

Don't get distracted from your original assignment. Too many Christians get so caught up in controversial issues that they lose their focus on reaching the world with a message of hope. Yes, politics, culture, poverty, social problems, media and a host of other issues are vitally important, but we need to keep them in the perspective of the Great Commission. Don't get distracted from your original calling.

One movie or TV show isn't going to bring down the faith that transformed the world. As I said in some of my interviews, this movie won't create a nation of agnostics or atheists. Yes, some will be duped; but frankly, the Christian faith defeated the Roman Empire and transformed music, literature, the arts, scholarship and science throughout Europe and the West. Although I'm always ready to share my faith, and I'm concerned about the moral decay of the culture, I'm not too worried that God really needs defending. He's done pretty well since the creation of the world. I think He'd rather have me spend more time focusing on loving my neighbor.

Individual believers need to be active in politics, from our local communities to the national level. But we must be very careful not to use our perceived political clout as a club. A far better way is to engage the culture, and the most hopeful method is through telling a powerful brand story.

Our ultimate goal is to win their hearts, and that only comes from inside.

Your brand will grow and succeed only if it deserves it. If your brand is connecting to the audience, giving their lives meaning and helping them accomplish their goals in life, then it will continue to sustain its impact.

I close this book with a quote from, of all people, Charles Darwin, the man whose theory of evolution has caused so much chaos, conflict and concern during the last century. I'm not a scientist, but I do know that whatever you think of his theories, Darwin got at least one thing right:

> It is not the strongest of the species that survive, nor the most intelligent, but rather the one most responsive to change.

Change happens, and change is coming whether we like it or not. We can bemoan modern advertising and marketing, criticize those who are pioneering new ideas, or turn our backs on new technology. Jesus criticized the Pharisees for not recognizing the signs of the times, and yet 2,000 years later, leaders of churches, ministries and nonprofits are still just as blind.

Creating an effective brand story doesn't mean being *reflexive* to the culture; it means being *responsive* to the culture—recognizing the change and being there with the story that has transformed so many generations before us.

Don't give your audience what you think they want. Give them what they never dreamed possible.

ENDNOTES

Prologue: Responding to a Media-driven Culture

1. James Twitchell, *Branded Nation* (New York: Simon and Schuster, 2005).

Introduction: Losing Our Voice

1. James Twitchell, *Branded Nation* (New York: Simon and Schuster, 2005), p. 47.
2. Robert E. Litan, "Innovators Matter Most," *The Wall Street Journal,* February 24-25, 2007, sec. A, p. 8.
3. Twitchell, *Branded Nation*, p. 59.
4. Douglas B. Sosnick, Matthew J. Dowd and Ron Fournier, *Appplebee's America: How Successful Political, Business, and Religious Leaders Connect with the New American Community* (New York: Simon and Schuster, 2006), p. 2.

Chapter One: Living in a Media-driven Culture

1. Michael J. Wolf, *The Entertainment Economy: How Mega-Media Forces Are Transforming Our Lives* (New York: Times Books, 1999), p. 4.
2. Marty Neumeister, *The Brand Gap* (Berkeley, CA: Peachpit Press, 2005), p. 40.
3. "Television and Health," California State University Northridge, data compiled by TV-Free America. http://www.csun.edu/science/health/docs/tv&health.html (accessed November 2007).
4. Ibid.
5. Denise Gellene, "Teens Who Use Cell Phones Most Found to Be Sadder and Less Assured," *Los Angeles Times,* May 24, 2006 (reporting on a meeting of the American Psychiatric Association in Toronto).
6. James Twitchell, *Branded Nation* (New York: Simon & Schuster Paperbacks, 2005), p. 2.

Chapter Four: A New Religion

1. Wally Olins, *Wally Olins on B®and* (New York: Thames and Hudson, 2003), p. 11.
2. Tom Boudoin, *Consuming Faith: Integrating Who We Are with What We Buy* (Lanham, MD: Sheed and Ward, 2003), p. xiii.
3. George Barna, personal interview with the author, November 2007.
4. Patrick Hanlon, *Primal Branding* (New York: Free Press, 2006), pp. 9-85.
5. Ibid., p. 70.
6. Linda Tischler, "How Do I Love Thee? Let Me Plot the Graph," *Fast Company,* July 2004, no. 84, p. 64.
7. Martin Lindstrom, "Religion: Inspiration for Brands," The Branding Strategy Insider, May 4, 2007. http://www.brandingstrategyinsider.com/2007/05/religion_inspir.html#more (accessed November 2007).
8. Ibid.

Chapter Five: Telling Your Story

1. Peter Montoya with Tim Vandehey, *The Brand Called You* (Tustin, CA: Personal Branding Press, 2003), pp. 42-43,53.
2. Ibid., p. 41.
3. America Online Poll, November 9, 2006.

Chapter Six: The Right Branding Tools

1. Douglas B. Sosnick, Matthew J. Dowd and Ron Fournier, *Applebee's America: How Successful Political, Business and Religious Leaders Connect with the New American Community* (New York: Simon and Schuster, 2006), p. 65.
2. Neil Postman, *Amusing Ourselves to Death* (New York: Penguin Books, 1985), p. 7.
3. Malcolm Muggeridge, *Christ and the Media* (Grand Rapids, MI: William B. Eerdmans Publishing Co., 1977), p. 64.
4. Ibid., p. 106.
5. Ibid., p. 58.
6. Sosnick, Dowd and Fournier, *Applebee's America: How Successful Political, Business and Religious Leaders Connect with the New American Community*, p. 69.

Chapter Seven: Great Design

1. Virginia Postral, *The Substance of Style: How the Rise of Aesthetic Value Is Remaking Commerce, Culture, and Consciousness* (New York: Harper Perennial, 2004), p. 2.
2. D. K. Holland, *Branding for Non-Profits: Developing Identity with Integrity* (New York: Allworth Press, 2006), p. 71.

Chapter Eight: The Dark Side of Branding

1. Mercer Schuchardt, "Swooshtika: Icons for Corporate Tribes," September 13, 2002. http://www.theooze.com/articles/article.cfm?id=132 (accessed November 2006).
2. "Google Signs $900 Million News Corp Deal," BBC News, August 7, 2006. http://news.bbc.co.uk/2/hi/business/5254642.stm. Steve Rubel, "MySpace Mania," Micro Persuasion, March 30, 2006. http://www.micropersuasion.com/2006/03/myspace_mania.html.
3. Ely Portillo, "Loneliness Looks Popular These Days," Knight Ridder News Service, June 23, 2006. http://www.signonsandiego.com/uniontrib/20060623/news_1n23lonely.html (accessed November 2007).
4. Ibid.
5. Shane Hipps, *The Hidden Power of Electronic Culture* (Grand Rapids, MI: Zondervan, 2005), p. 112.
6. Janet Kornblum, "Meet My 5,000 New Best Pals," *USA Today*, September 19, 2006. http://www.usatoday.com/tech/news/2006-09-19-friending_x.htm (accessed November 2007).
7. Neil Postman, *Amusing Ourselves to Death* (New York: Penguin Books, 1985), pp. vii-viii.
8. Erwin McManus, speech to National Religious Broadcasters Conference (February 18, 2007), Orlando, FL.
9. Robyn Waters, *The Trendmaster's Guide: Get a Jump on What Your Customer Wants Next* (New York: Penguin Group, 2005), p. xi.
10. Ibid.
11. Os Guiness, *Prophetic Untimeliness* (Grand Rapids, MI: Baker Books, 2005), p. 65.
12. Philip Denneson and James Street, *Selling Out the Church* (Nashville, TN: Abingdon Press, 1997), p. 143.
13. Dictionary.com, s.v. "marketing." http://dictionary.reference.com/browse/marketing (accessed November 2006).
14. Investopedia.com, "Marketing." http://www.Investopedia.com. http://www.investopedia.com/terms/m/marketing.asp (accessed November 2006).
15. Ibid.
16. Robert F. Lusch, "Marketing's Evolving Identity: Defining Our Future," American Marketing Association. http://www.marketingpower.com/content2018879.php (accessed November 2007).

17. Walter Brueggemann, *Biblical Perspectives on Evangelism: Living in a Three Storied Universe* (Nashville, TN: Abingdon Press, 1993), p. 88.

Chapter Nine: The Branding Imperative

1. Wally Olins, *Wally Olins on B®and* (New York: Thames and Hudson, 2004), p. 89.
2. Jim Collins, *Good to Great in the Social Sectors* (Boulder, CO: Jim Collins, 2005), p. 2.
3. Ibid., p. 25.
4. Erik Du Plessis, *The Advertised Mind* (Sterling, VA: Millward Brown and Kogan Page Limited, 2005), p. 197.
5. Ibid., p. 118.
6. Ibid., p. 114.

Chapter Ten: The Future of Branding Faith

1. Malcolm Gladwell, *The Tippping Point* (New York: Back Bay Books, 2002), p. 132.

About the Author

According to former CNN journalist Paula Zahn, filmmaker and media strategist Phil Cooke is rare—he's a working producer in Hollywood with a Ph.D. in Theology. *Christianity Today* magazine has called him a "media guru," and his blog at philcooke.com is considered one of the most insightful resources on the web on issues of faith, culture, and media.

Through his company, Cooke Pictures, based in Los Angeles, California, Phil's team advises many of the largest and most effective nonprofit and faith-based media organizations in the world. He also speaks at workshops, seminars and conferences on a global basis. Phil has appeared on MSNBC, CNBC, CNN, and his work has been profiled in the *New York Times, The Los Angeles Times* and *The Wall Street Journal.*

For more information about how Cooke Pictures can impact your organization or project, check out their website at cookepictures.com.